How To Share Your Own Personal Data
Survive & Thrive In The Modern Data Economy

How To Share Your Own Personal Data
Survive & Thrive In The Modern Data Economy

Allan Simpson

On Data Privacy Ltd
2019

First Printing: 2019

ISBN 978-0-244-45845-4

On Data Privacy Ltd
Suite 342, 8 Church Street
Inverness, Scotland, United Kingdom IV1 1EA

www.ondataprivacy.com

Ordering Information:
Special discounts are available on quantity purchases by corporations, associations, educators, and others. For details, contact the publisher at the above listed address.

Trade bookstores and wholesalers: Please contact On Data Privacy Ltd

Tel: (+44) 1463 717115or email as@ondataprivacy.com

Dedication

In memory of my Dad, who taught me the value of maintaining discretion and dignity when dealing with other people.

Contents

Preface

Your personal data matters to you and is at the same time of value to others. Good or bad, they all want to use your personal data.

While the data privacy and protection industry feels, sounds and looks as though it is concentrating on technology solutions, in reality this is a people problem.

It is the how people behave which introduces the risk of harm coming to you as something goes wrong with your personal data.

People will cause accidents; people will behave illegally, people will be incompetent and people will be careless.

In relying too heavily on technology to solve the problems of data privacy all we do is invite it to accelerate the effects of the accidental, illegal, incompetent and careless. The sheer power of simple, "copy and paste" will see to that.

Part of the answer to the question of *"how do we protect our personal data in this modern data economy?"* lies in our own behaviour as individuals.

You and I need to understand how best to protect ourselves, then actually do it.

When we do so, we can increase our own personal value within this modern data economy. Not just surviving the threats but thriving on the benefits it can bring to us all.

Allan Simpson

Introduction

This book is about you.

It is about you and your personal data.

Your own relationship with your personal data, how you can make use of this personal data to your advantage and how to protect your data privacy.

Recent changes to European data protection law and regulation have put you in charge of your personal data. You now exercise a certain amount of control over how it is used. Whether this personal data is used online or offline doesn't matter. The new rules make the point that your personal data is yours. It belongs to you. You now have new rights over how it is used.

We will be discussing what those rights are. We will be looking at the responsibilities other people and organisations now have towards you.

All with a view to helping you do one thing in as safe an environment as possible.

To play your role in the modern data economy.

Some call it a "digital economy". I think this is misleading. You see, "digital" describes just one way your personal data can be recorded, moved, copied, shared, stored and deleted.
There is also, for want of a better way of putting it, "analogue". For me, the term analogue describes what we did before digital took over so much of our lives.

Which means paper records, notebooks, photocopies, reading printed books, meeting face to face, newspapers, postcards, letters, telephone calls and writing things down on a piece of paper.

All the things we did before digital. And we still do them to this day. Usually digital has changed the way we use analogue. Sometimes people are resolutely analogue in defiance of digital. Your personal data is now processed using a combination of digital and analogue techniques.

Your Identity

Your personal data is important to you because it combines to form your identity. We shall look at "identity" in more detail shortly. For now, it might help if you think about the fact you use parts of your identity to take enable your daily life. The real purpose of this book is to help you understand that every time you interact in this modern data economy you are both making use of your identity *and* exposing it to risk. You indulge in the former and hope to avoid the latter.

Today, it is easy for others to misuse or even steal parts of your identity. Have you considered what life would be like if someone stole your identity?

The Modern Data Economy

The common factor between analogue and digital is that both are used to collect, store, handle and share our personal data. The modern data economy relies upon both for success. It is now rare

Allan Simpson

for us to collect our purchase, hand over a fistful of cash and walk away, ending the relationship there.

Without a means of collecting, storing, handling and sharing our personal data, we cannot transact with other people and organisations. The modern data economy makes use of both analogue and digital systems to do so.

And so dear reader, I give you the modern data economy. It is now the way the world works and each of us needs to make adjustments to make it work for us.

This World Is Full Of Contrasts

The modern data economy is capable of helping us all as individuals join together to achieve amazing acts of kindness and positive results. At the same time it is capable of focusing the collective wrath of the many against the few.

The modern data economy can bring together a range of factors to help protect us and make us feel safer. At the same time it contains a constant, permanent threat we must be aware of if we are to prevent it from bringing our lives to a halt.

If you are to play your part in this modern data economy – as buyer, seller, participant, observer, manufacturer, explorer, employer, employee, analyst, regulator or influencer – you need to understand how and when to deploy your personal data in a way which protects your privacy.
It is *your* personal data which is the key to taking part in the modern data economy. It has become almost impossible for you to take part without it.

Almost. Yet operating outside of the data economy takes a lot of effort.

The combination of good and bad surrounding each and every transaction within the modern data economy means you need to exercise a level of awareness, caution, scepticism and skill in order to look after your own safety.

Develop some of those skills and you can enjoy the "good" the data economy has to offer. Fail to understand the need for awareness, caution, scepticism and skill and you dramatically increase your risk of experiencing the "bad".

Is This A Useful Analogy?

A Comparison With The Responsibility Of Driving A Car

In some ways, using your own personal data as part of your daily life is like driving a car.

There are written rules about how you should drive a car. For example: Which side of the road you should use; how many people can be safely seated; wearing a seatbelt; being aware of the environment around you; what is considered safe and unsafe (for example texting whilst driving) or how fast you can go.

You have to pass a driving test in order to be trusted with using a car on the road and to confirm your basic understanding of the rules.

Then there are unwritten rules which are no less sensible: Parking straight and not using two parking bays; the importance of locking your car; cleaning and maintaining it from time to time; adding oil, water and fuel or checking the tyres.

You only really learn about these aspects of driving after you pass your test. Indeed sometimes you only learn their value by learning the hard way.

If you're a car owner, you make use of all these rules and many more as you make your way from A to B and back again every day.

The Responsibility Of Owning Your Personal Data

Owning your personal data also carries responsibilities. However unlike owning a car, the rules and regulations apply to those who want to make use of your personal data. They don't really apply to you as an individual.

Which means many of us are either self-taught or untrained when it comes to sharing our personal data and looking after our own privacy.

We can't keep it all to ourselves or we will never leave A on the way to B. Yet we *must* move from A to B. We must make use of our personal data if we are to consume goods and services, go to work, donate to a just giving page or book a holiday.

So every day we take to the, "modern data economy road", without a standard level of awareness or competence. We have all the power to choose but few of the skills and little of the experience necessary to make good choices. We are at risk.

As it is based on the decisions we take, this risk is of our own making. Yet it is different from the risk we run when we drive a car on the open road.

In a car, we can choose not to wear a seatbelt, to break the speed limit, to text our friends or check our email on the move.

The rules say we shouldn't do it. However we can choose to be irresponsible. Some of us do these things anyway. A few of us do them all at the same time. We run the risk of:

1. Getting caught and,
2. Something really nasty happening to us.

These risks are reduced if we take responsibility for our actions and play by the rules, observing the speed limit, putting on our seat belt and leaving the smartphone alone.

When sharing our own personal data, the written rules and regulations don't apply to us when we share our own details.

Only unwritten rules apply. There are things we should and shouldn't do if we are to share our own personal data relatively safely. The written rules are for other people and organisations. Aren't they?

You and I have the choice to take responsibility for our data sharing behaviour or not. We have the choice to self-educate about data privacy or remain ignorant. You can *choose* to share your personal data in an obviously hazardous environment. You can *choose* to accept the risks or even to ignore their implications.

Unlike taking risks when driving a car, the risks when sharing your personal data are with you *all the time*. This is the unacceptable face of the modern data economy. It sits on your shoulder and waits for the right moment.

There is always someone looking to take advantage of your carelessness or ignorance. You can drive in an unsafe manner for years without anything bad ever happening to you. Yet you can't take similar risks with your personal data and expect to go unscathed.

The personal data threat is everywhere. It is not constrained by distance or proximity. You can take all the positive, safe practice advice available and still be unlucky and affected by a seemingly unconnected data breach in systems you never even knew existed. In the modern data economy you might not suffer from only one crash. You can be really unlucky and crash in lots of places at the same time, then repeat crashing until all your resources have withered away and there's nothing left.

Safe use of your personal requires this of you:

1. That you take responsibility for your own behaviours.

2. That you actively hold to account those with whom you share your data.

3. That you invoke your rights over how your personal data is used.

In the absence of a "personal data driving test" the onus is on you to take responsibility for how you share your personal data. This landed on your shoulders the day you were given the power to choose. You have new rights over how your personal data is used. If they are to work to your benefit in the modern data economy, the responsibility is yours. Let me explain how this works.

How To Share Your Own Personal Data

Chapter 1

What Is Personal Data?

One of the slightly confusing aspects of the new Data Protection regulations is they refer to "personal data" in terms intended for use by the people and organisations who will process it. Not in terms you or I, as the people who actually own our personal data, might recognise.

So the first thing we need to do is rectify that.

It helps to think of Personal Data as being on one of four categories:

a) Data which IS you (eg. your name)

b) Data which is ABOUT you (eg. your marital status)

c) Data which illustrates your behaviour and preferences (eg. what you do, like, dislike and believe);

d) Data which is connected to you (eg. your driving license number)

If I asked you to list as many items of your own personal data as you can think of, right now, how many could you come up with?

Remember, this new regulation – the General Data Protection Regulation (GDPR) gives you powerful rights over your personal data. It is yours. You own the right whether or not to share it with anyone else. How many items can you think of?

Here is the list I came up with. It is not a definitive list, there are bound to be other items I haven't considered yet, feel free to add your own:

Items Of Personal Data – An Example List

- First name
- Middle name(s)
- Last name
- Maiden name
- Other names used
- Username
- Personal email address
- Work email address
- Photographs of your face
- Other identifying photographs
- Photo location data (as recorded by a smartphone camera)
- Video footage
- Voice recording
- Password
- Security question & answer
- Cookies
- Date of birth

- City of birth
- Birth certificate
- Age
- Weight
- Height
- Gender
- Eye colour
- Hair colour
- Work address
- Current home address
- Length of time at current address
- Previous addresses
- Home phone number
- Mobile phone number
- Work phone number
- Marital status
- Spouse name
- Parents' names
- Children's names
- Siblings' names
- Friends' names

- Contacts list
- Pets names
- Number of people in your household
- Awards or decorations received
- Occupation
- Current employer
- Employment history
- Performance evaluations
- Reference interviews
- HR issues & disciplinary actions
- IP address
- Internet Service Provider (ISP)
- Device ID / MAC address
- Browser
- Operating system
- Language preference
- Social media accounts
- Social media posts & history
- Cloud storage files
- Current location (physical)
- Location history (physical)

- Shopping & purchase history (on a website)
- Transaction history (elsewhere online)
- Shopping & purchase history (offline)
- Daily life activities
- Event attendance
- Donations to organisations
- Donations to people
- Payments to people
- Media preferences
- Likes & ratings
- Topics of interest
- Activity on a website
- Search history on a website
- Search history on a search engine
- Browsing history
- Phone call records
- Text message history
- Messages on a website
- Chat history - Skype, Messenger, Whatsapp, etc
- Email records
- Postal activity

- Current income
- Income history
- PAYE information
- Employee reference number
- Bank account
- Credit card number
- Debit card number
- Loyalty card number
- PIN number
- Credit report
- Loan records
- Other financial statements
- Home owned or rented
- Home value
- Investment records
- Property records
- Life insurance records
- Health insurance records
- Pension records
- National Insurance number
- Car insurance records

- Passport information
- Social security records
- Driving licence
- Vehicle registration records
- Membership of a Professional organisation
- Membership of a Trade Union
- Membership of a club
- Voter registration records
- Council Tax registration
- Political party affiliation
- Fingerprints
- Handwriting
- Signature
- Writing sample (electronic)
- Schools attended
- Education history
- Arrest records
- Bankruptcies
- Judgements
- Criminal offences & convictions
- Pardons

- Tax returns
- Racial & ethnic origin
- Nationality
- Political opinions
- Religion & philosophical beliefs
- Sexual orientation
- Sexual partners
- Medical records
- Allergies
- Family health history
- Prescriptions
- Physical or mental disability
- Military service record
- Genetic information
- Biometric identifiers
- Retina scan
- Voice signature
- Facial geometry
- Product warranty/ownership registrations
- Your permission or authorisation to access systems at work

How did you get on with your own list?

There are more than 130 items of personal data listed here. Their value to you is immeasurable: Some of these items, if you were to lose them, have them taken from you or misused by someone else, simply could not be replaced.

When combined, they form your own personal identity. They are *you*.

Their value to others depends on the items and combinations they are able to access. A handful of the items listed above can unlock the other items.

To take part in the modern data economy you need to share selected items with other people and organisations and allow them to "process" your personal data. In exchange for which you should expect to get something of value in return.

Some of these items of personal data form the keys to access everything else a data thief needs to make your life miserable. If they are able to combine them in a format suitable for their purposes, you can find yourself in trouble.

What Does "Processing" Personal Data Mean?

If an organisation, no matter how small, takes items of your personal data and does any of the following with it, they are processing it:

- Obtain it
- Record it
- Hold it

- Manipulate it

- Organise it

- Retrieve it

- Adapt, alter or modify it

- Use it

- Transmit it

- Destroy it

- Erase it

(Note, personal data processed in the course of a purely personal or household activity is not covered by GDPR, so you can still send Birthday cards to your relatives and friends without worrying...)

Some organisations and businesses have not yet reached a clear understanding of which items of your personal data their either process or want to process. Many are still not clear about what processing actually means.

In the modern data economy, where you need to share your personal data if you're going to make it work for you, this is something you should be concerned about.

If an organisation wants to process your personal data they need to have a "lawful reason" for processing it. If they don't have this, they are breaking the law and putting you at personal risk. You need to be able to protect yourself.

How Your Personal Data Can Be Deployed

There are 8 ways in which your personal data can be deployed:

1. You can share it with other people and organisations in order to allow transactions between you to be carried out in a safe, transparent manner and nothing goes wrong.

2. You can share it with other people and organisations in order to allow transactions between you to be carried out in a safe, transparent manner and something goes wrong by accident "internally" (within the responsibility of whoever you shared it with).

3. You can share it with other people and organisations in order to allow transactions between you to be carried out in a safe, transparent manner and something goes wrong by deliberate action internally.

4. You can share your personal data with other people and organisations and it is intercepted or diverted to a third party who seeks to use it for their own purpose.

5. Your personal data is shared by you as a result of deception by the recipient.

6. Your personal data is accessed without your knowledge.

7. Your personal data is accessed because of your own negligence.

8. Your personal data is accessed because of your own ignorance.

The 9th possibility is a situation where your personal data exists but isn't shared or accessed by anyone. Which means nobody else can use it, but neither can you. In effect, nothing happens. In the modern data economy this just isn't feasible. You exist, you have personal data around you. Yet you need to be able to access it if you are to interact with society in a meaningful way.

The ideal situation is for your personal data to be accessed, or perhaps "borrowed" by someone in exchange for the value (goods and services they offer) in a controlled manner. When the value exchange is completed, the personal data is returned/released to you. You might think of your personal data as a token which allows an exchange of value to happen.

When your personal data is under your control and is processed in an environment where transparency and trust exists, it is likely the personal data will be returned to you in good condition, ready to be used again.

When your personal data is introduced to an unsafe environment, either by the actions of others or as a result of your own decisions or behaviours. Your personal data can be compromised, altered, infected or rendered useless. Which means you lose control over how it is to be used or it can never use it again. Then harm can come to you.

Harm takes a variety of forms in this context. From minor irritation to life changing consequences.

It is a fact of the modern data economy that the threat of harm as a result of the misuse of your personal data is *constant*.

EU governments have introduced a regulation to help protect you from harm as a result of misuse of your personal data. It's called the EU General Data Protection Regulation (GDPR) – part of the Data Protection Act 2018 in the UK.

This book is about helping you to understand how to benefit from it as a private individual. How to make use of the new rights and responsibilities to make sure you are able to use your data to take advantage of the modern data economy - and to ensure those who wish to make use of your personal data do so in a way which protects you.

Why Your Personal Data Matters

It Belongs To You

Your personal data matters because it is yours. You own it.

You were born with some of it. The rest of it you picked up over the years. You either collected it yourself or it was given to you as you worked through the education system, entered into the world of work, earned money, saved it, spent it, rented or bought your home, attended your local GP or hospital.

Everything which describes you and your path through life to date is your personal data. It can be used to identify you as an individual. It is your identity.

Data Gathers Around You

Yet there is another side to your personal data. It is the personal data which all those interactions have created about you. It is lurking. You might not be aware of it. Some organisations have forgotten they had it. But it is still there.

Other organisations make regular use of it to target you, to create a profile about you. This kind of personal data often identifies you indirectly. Records of what you buy, what you like, where you were, what you did, who you called, who called you and whether or not you responded to a particular issue.

When these two sides are combined, your personal data has additional value to organisations. It means they know not just who and where you are, but what you do, what you like and what you are likely to respond to. They themselves seek to extract part of this value for their own purposes. Which can be as simple as trying to sell you something or as sinister as trying to influence your voting habits, to blackmail you, to steal from you or to access something of value to you, such as the contents of your bank account.

The effect of this is you buy something, you change your behaviour and attitude or you succumb to overwhelming pressure. In our world today organisations, both friendly and unfriendly, can use your own personal data to make you do any of these things. Without ever knowing you or meeting you.

If they can access your data, even little scraps of it, they can start a process to influence your thoughts and behaviour.

This can be benign and useful to you, perhaps in the form of marketing communication. Or it can be hostile and dangerous in the hands of criminals, rogue governments or simply used by people who don't like you.

Your personal data matters to them. They need access to your personal data in order to achieve *their* objectives.

This kind of personal data can also be used to identify you as an individual.

Your personal data *should* matter to you. You need it in order to have the freedom to live your life the way you want. If you want to take advantage of the goods and services on offer, if you want to interact with society in general and take part in the modern data economy, if you want to apply for a job or open a bank account, you need your personal data.

It is yours. You own it. It is time to make sure you look after it.

Understanding The Modern Data Economy

Locally, nationally and internationally, the economy now relies upon the ability to transfer and process personal data.

It is increasingly difficult to do anything without leaving a little trail of personal data behind you. The simplest of tasks can involve the transmission, collection and sharing of your own personal data.

Consider simply walking down to your local shop to buy a pint of milk and a loaf of bread:

- You might be captured on local government operated CCTV in the street on the way there. Recording your image and location.

- You will probably be captured by individual business CCTV as you walk into and move around the shop. Also recording your image and location.

- You might pay for your purchase using your contactless bank card. Recording your name and payment details.

- If you have a loyalty card for the shop, you probably use it. Recording your name, location, the amount you spent and your purchase preferences.

- Your smartphone records your every move with its location tracking. Recording your location, journey and the places you visited, together with information about any texts, calls or personal messages you may have made during the journey. Some of this data may be attached to your social media account in a way which makes it visible to others.

You can see from this example that even in the simple act of buying your food for the day, information about you, what you do, when you do it, what you like and where you are, is being recorded.

Your face, the clothes you wore, who you spoke to in the shop, the shelves you browsed, who you bank with, the type of card you use, your shopping preferences, your location, the time of your visit, the duration of your visit, the start and end points of your journey.

All recorded as a matter of course.

Where does it all go? How is this data going to be used? By whom? What do they know about you?

Even simple transactions cause simple data to be collected. The transactions rely upon certain parts of this data or they don't happen. You can't buy a pint of milk without going into the shop and paying for it. Of course you can do some of it anonymously (pay in cash for example), but as the transactions increase in size, frequency, complexity, scale, scope or distance, the use of personal data makes it easier for them to happen because it is easier for you to use.

Your contactless payment card is an example. Your personal data is carried on the card and is used to create a transaction when you wave the card over a reader. It is so much easier than using cash. Would it be churlish of me to suggest the banks have invested heavily in making contactless technology so easy to use because it is so much cheaper for them to operate than cash? Possibly. But I'd still be correct.

The banks have altered your behaviour away from anonymous cash and towards a transaction process driven by technology and personal data. There are good, positive reasons for doing so. The benefits of ease of use for you, efficiency for both you and the bank and the fact that less actual cash is put at risk are good reasons for going contactless. It all works very well as long as the personal data involved is safeguarded.

The more complex the transaction, the more personal data processing is needed to ensure it works properly. For both the vendor and for you.

If data can't move relatively freely, the transactions can't happen with the necessary speed or accuracy and the economy falters as a result.

Which means the ability to purchase goods and services is curtailed, their delivery is slower or less accurate, queues or backlogs form and the value to both the supplier and customer is reduced. On top of which, the cost per transaction increases. The value of each transaction is squeezed on all sides. Which results in less value for all of us.

The modern data economy needs the movement of personal data to be as friction-free as possible. Some governments deliberately introduce friction by controlling or denying the flow of data to suit their own purposes. Others recognise and understand the benefits of smooth, safe transfers of personal data over national borders.

Allan Simpson

The need for security, data protection and privacy can also introduce elements of friction. In order for the flow of data to move as easily as possible, it needs to be processed in an appropriate way. In a way which protects the data, and the people who own it, from harm. In a way which reduces risk. Otherwise, if the people who own the data feel the risks involved are too great, they will reduce or even cease the flow of data. And the economy grinds to a halt.

You and I, as the owners of our own personal data, each contribute to the global economy. We do it with our personal data.

The Harsh Realities

As data is processed, it is subject to risk. Processing data (we'll look at what this really means in more detail shortly) makes it susceptible to interference, loss, damage and errors.

Harsh Reality Number 1 – Criminal Activity

The first harsh reality is that because the modern data economy relies upon the free movement of personal data, there are those who seek to take advantage of this. They want to intercept the personal data owned by you and I and extract the value for themselves.

You read about them in the press. "Hackers" or "Data thieves". They can be working on their own, as part of organised crime or even as part of rogue government action. The attacks vary from sophisticated use of significant technical resources to an individual simply typing your email address and "password1234" into the login page of a website.

They cause "data breaches". When they access, copy and divert your personal data from a trusted system into an untrustworthy one *they* control. They can wreak havoc with your bank account or simply share your deepest secrets on social media with anyone interested. Each of us has something we are sensitive about. It is not always the case that financial loss is the worst thing which could happen to you. Embarrassment or loss of face can have dreadful consequences. Revealing sensitive information can cause an individual to become isolated and vulnerable.

Harsh Reality Number 2 – Accidents Will Happen

The second harsh reality is that many data breaches are not caused by criminals. Instead they are caused by accidents, incompetence, negligence, carelessness, lack of awareness, an absence of training, inadequate systems or inept management.

In the news media you only get to read about the high-profile data breaches. Those involving multinational companies such as airlines, global hotel chains or banks and involving the records of tens of thousands of customers at a time. Whilst it is good to see large organisations being held to account when things go wrong, the number of breaches involving thousands of records is dwarfed by the number of breaches involving one or a handful of records.

Yet because you read about massive data breach and the threat of huge consequential fines in the news media, it all seems far removed from your own life. However, Harsh Reality Number 2 tells you the following types of data breach are happening every hour of every day.

Papers go missing, documents get coffee spilt on them or are filed incorrectly - never to be seen again. Computer hard drives get corrupted and the data stored on them is lost. Laptops get stolen or left on a train, mobile phones are dropped down the toilet. Archive storage gets flooded. Computer servers fail and make the data stored upon them inaccessible. USB drives are used to make copies of personal data for someone to take home to work on over the weekend. Each of these could be happening to your personal data every day.

People make mistakes. A typing or filing error can make the records attached to a document lost to those searching for them. Copies of personal data can be made and distributed without any thought given to the risks involved, just because it didn't cross anyone's mind to consider them.

The combination of Harsh Realities means that data breaches are inevitable. They will happen either because of a deliberate or accidental action. They can affect only one record or one hundred thousand records. The risks might be mitigated (reduced) or they could be profound and threaten harm to one or many of us. The threat to the integrity of digital systems is constant because some people can use intelligence and systems to automate the threat and apply it in many places. The threat to everything else is constant because people in general (which means you and I) don't use their own intelligence. We fall into lazy habits, we take short cuts, we become arrogant, careless or remain ignorant. We fail to implement safe practice.

Yes. People are as much a threat to your personal data as technology. Each is bad enough on their own. Imagine what it's like when the two are multiplied together...

The harsh reality of life, certainly of life with the modern data economy, is that there are now not just two but three certainties:

Death, Taxes and Data Breaches.

The problem with the certainty of a data breach happening at some point, is that the risk of it happening can threaten trust in the processing of personal data. An absence of trust means people are less willing to submit their personal data, which introduces friction to the processing and transfer of personal data. Reducing the flow and with it the economic benefit.

If we all fear a breach so much that we keep our personal data to ourselves, the modern data economy falls flat on its face.

Harsh Reality Number 3 – You Can Never Be 100% Protected

In the period since the GDPR came into effect, the need for such a regulation has become abundantly clear.

Organisations all over the world have proved to us all that 100% assurance of the protection or privacy of personal data is impossible.

It is not just the skills and resources available to organised criminals or the actions of rogue governments which cause this. It is the fact that many organisations aren't doing a good enough job of understanding what is required. Some apply their own jaundiced interpretation of the modern data economy. Others regard investment in data protection and security as one with "no upside". In which case they are choosing to ignore the benefits of transparency and trust.

I think it is fair to suggest that none of us expect 100% protection and privacy. We live in a society where criminals can operate and accidents will happen even if we take every digital device out of the equation. We need to be realistic.

Instead, what all of us should be entitled to expect is this: A basic level of awareness and capability is exercised by other people and organisations who would seek to make use of our personal data for an authorised purpose.

We know we can't keep criminals out all the time. Yet we still use basic protection methods such as locking our front door, just to make it that little bit more difficult for them to take advantage of us. Which illustrates to me that as private individuals we still have some faith in a basic level of protection.

Apply this to the modern data economy and what you see should worry you.

This basic level of security, protection and privacy assurance is only being applied in thin layers and patches. The business world has not yet bought in to the concept of a reward from you in exchange for providing you with some evidence proving they take the privacy of your personal data seriously.

They all want your personal data but are reluctant to prove they are worthy of it.

Airlines, hotel chains, manufacturers and retailers have all recently proved it is impossible to be 100% secure. Understanding this and making allowances for it, what matters to you and I is their ability to reduce the threat of harm to us when an incident does occur. Some of them are better at this than others.

Whilst it is unreasonable for us to expect 100% security and protection, we should be able to expect 100% effort made to uphold our rights as data subjects. To date, not all that many organisations are making such an effort.

Is There A "But..."?

Yes there is. If we each act in our individual capacity. If we take responsibility to look after *our own* personal data and *our own* interests. If we expect others who want to make use of our personal data to live up to *our* standards. Then we can all chip away at the human factors which cause fixable errors.

If we each take the opportunity to invoke our rights. If we are each alive to the behaviours the GDPR seeks to change in terms of data processing. Then we might achieve something, collectively and as individuals.

On an individual basis, if nothing else, at least your own personal data will be that little bit safer.

Mind you, taking on the multinationals and the huge data processors? That's a different matter altogether. Acting as individuals we can't expect to influence their behaviour. However if we start to act as a movement, applying new standards and expectations of privacy management, then we can start to encourage change. Change which each of us is able to reward, creating the "upside" which can change organisational decision making when it comes to privacy decisions.

Well I can dream can't I?

Let's start with what we *can* influence.

Chapter 2

The New Regulations

Governments, particularly governments in the European Union (EU) were aware of the issues surrounding data processing in the modern digital economy and sought to take action to ensure personal data can flow as freely as possible in as safe a manner as possible. They recognised that data processing can only work for the economy if it can be trusted by those involved. And so a new regulation was developed and introduced.

The General Data Protection Regulation or GDPR. In the UK this regulation informs the Data Protection Act 2018, which contains, amongst other things, the full GDPR.

There are other regulations which affect the way your personal data is processed. One we'll consider in this book is the Privacy and Electronic Communications Regulation or PECR as it is sometimes known.

An upgrade to PECR is likely within the next two years. The EU is currently working on a draft ePrivacy regulation. However as we don't know enough about what this will look like when the various EU bodies have finished arguing about it, I'm not going to go into much detail.

About GDPR

The GDPR is a major upgrade to data protection regulation. In the UK the Data Protection Act it replaced was introduced in 1998. As you can imagine, a lot has changed in twenty years. The internet is completely different nowadays. Phenomena such as social media and iPhones didn't exist in 1998. The behaviours then compared to the behaviours in this decade were completely different and the old regulation was not fit for purpose.

The GDPR represents an attempt by regulators to apply some rigour to the protection and privacy of personal data in the modern data economy. A fairly good effort it is too, in my opinion. It has its flaws and detractors but for me, these are people who are failing to see the opportunities it can bring to all of us. And especially to you and I as the owners of our own personal data. The GDPR changes the balance of power in favour of you and I as private citizens. You and I are now entitled to ask, "...so what will this do for me?".

What This Means For You

The GDPR has granted you, as the owner of your own personal data, new and powerful rights. It puts you in control of what happens with your personal data. It gives you choice.

As long as you are: Alive, a "natural person" (ie, not a business entity) and are resident in the EU, You are now what the GDPR calls a "data subject".

(note: Brexit does not change this, the rights are now formed in British law)

As a data subject, you have rights over how your personal data can be used. Remember, there will be many occasions when you *want* your personal data to be used. However you want it to be used in a reliable and trustworthy way. Otherwise, if you stopped all use of your personal data, you wouldn't be able to buy anything without going to a shop and paying cash for it. Which isn't really how the modern economy works. Is it?

Whilst the EU has used the word "Protection" in the name of the regulation, it is really about the Privacy of your personal data. To my mind, data protection is part of data privacy. There are privacy considerations beyond "protection".

The Definition of Personal Data

The GDPR defines "personal data" as:

...any information relating to an identified or identifiable natural person ("data subject"); in identifiable natural person is one who can be identified, directly or indirectly, in particular by reference to an identifier such as a name, an identification number, location data, an online identifier or to one or more factors specific to the physical, physiological, genetic, mental, economic, cultural or social identity of that natural person;"

Whilst on the face of it this appears quite a mouthful, it is very clever.

You see, the GDPR is what is known as a "principles based" regulation. In other words, it sets out the overall ends the regulation is designed to achieve. How these ends are to be met in practice is down to others to interpret and achieve. Including enforcement and definition by either the national data protection authority (in the UK this is the Information Commissioner's Office or ICO) or a court of law. This definition is designed as a catch-all.

Allan Simpson

This has caused, as you might imagine, a bit of resentment amongst businesses without ready access to the specialist legal, data protection or privacy management skills necessary to meet the requirements of the regulation. It has also caused a great many interpretations about ways to comply with the regulation. Some are better than others, which is why you need to be aware of what is going on if you are to protect your own personal data.

Conversely it is also one of the flaws. Big organisations can afford all the legal people necessary to stay compliant with the regulation - or at least to argue their case when what they're doing turns out to be questionable. Smaller organisations can't. So it could be said there is a sort of "2-tier" regulation. One for the haves and another for the have-nots.

For our purposes as private individuals, we don't really care about that. The regulation is here. It gives us rights over how our personal data is collected and processed, regardless of the size of the data controller. We are more interested in deploying those rights to our benefit and for our personal safety.

Special Category Data

There is another classification of personal data which the GDPR calls "special category" data. This is personal data which could be of a sensitive nature and to which data controllers need to pay particular attention.

Processing of Special Category personal data is specifically prohibited by the GDPR unless conditions apply. Let's look at what is included in those special categories, then we'll look at the conditions which permit data controllers to process them.

Special categories of personal data are those which reveal:

- Racial or ethnic origin
- Political opinions
- Religious or philosophical beliefs
- Trade union membership
- The processing of genetic data or biometric data for the purpose of identifying a natural person
- Health data
- Data concerning a natural person's sex life or sexual orientation

Special category data contains examples of who you are, what you represent, what you stand for, what you believe in, where you have come from and aspects of your life which are simply facts pertinent to you which cannot be changed.

They are all examples of personal data which could be used to identify you, isolate you, bully you or used to reveal details about yourself you would rather be kept secret. In the wrong hands, or deployed in the wrong way, these items of personal data could be used to bring harm to you.

For this reason the GDPR requires data controllers to make sure one of several lawful reasons for processing applies. We'll consider these shortly.

What About Children's Data?

The GDPR does mention Children's data. Children are regarded as "vulnerable" in the context of processing personal data:

"Conditions applicable to child consent in relation to information Society services

Paragraph 4.8 of Article 6 applies in relation to the offer of information Society (which means social media) *services directly to a child the processing of the personal data of a child shall be lawful where the child is at least 16 years old where the child is below the age of 16 years such processing shall be lawful only if and to the extent that consent is given or authorised by the holder of parental responsibility over the child.*

The controller shall make reasonable efforts to verify in such cases that consent is given or authorised by the holder of parental responsibility over the child taking into consideration available technology."

While we're on the subject of definitions, there are a few others I need to introduce you to:

Data Controller - a definition

"...means the natural or legal person, public authority, agency or other body which, alone or jointly with others, determines the purposes and means of the processing of personal data; where the purposes and means of such processing are determined by Union or Member State law, the controller or the specific criteria for its nomination may be provided for by Union or Member State law;"

A data controller is the person or organisation which decides to collect and use (process) your personal data. From small businesses to government organisations, if they decide why the processing is to be done, they are a data controller and they have obligations to you. If you ever come to invoke your rights, you will be addressing this to the data controller.

A data controller can also carry out data processing.

Data Processor - a definition

"...means a natural or legal person, public authority, agency or other body which processes personal data on behalf of the controller;"

Data processors carry out processing for a data controller. The data processor is obliged to operate under instructions provided by the data controller and to help the data controller to uphold your rights.

Now this is important. Data controllers should tell you when they use data processors. Their use of a data processor should be governed by a contract between them. The purpose of this contract is to protect you.

Processing - a definition

The GDPR defines "processing" as:

"...any operation or set of operations which is performed on personal data or on sets of personal data, whether or not by automated means, such as collection, recording, organisation,

structuring, storage, adaptation or alteration, retrieval, consultation, use, disclosure by transmission, dissemination or otherwise making available, alignment or combination, restriction, erasure or destruction;"

I think it is important for you to understand exactly what "processing" means in the context of your personal data. This is a definition which is designed to capture all existing methods of processing: Online; offline; analogue and digital. It is also designed to work well into the future.

In essence, from the point at which a data controller collects your data until and including the conclusion of it being erased or destroyed, anything done to it is regarded as processing. This includes your personal data lying dormant in storage. So even if the data controller is doing nothing else with it, the fact they still have it is considered processing.

There is one small caveat you need to be aware of though. The data needs to be stored in an organised way, however rudimentary, in some sort of filing system. So if you deal with a tradesman for example, a painter or a carpenter, who keeps all his records on pieces of paper piled into a box or a bucket in no order at all, GDPR does not apply (you know these people exist, I've heard accountants griping about clients who arrive in the office with all their receipts in a bucket on the day their self-assessment tax return is due).
As soon as these papers are put into an alphabetical or date ordered filing system, GDPR applies. If the tradesman uses a computer of any kind to process their records, GDPR applies.

The problem for you is this. Some data controllers are deliberately woolly about their data processing. They don't like having to tell you the what, why, when and who else of their organisational processing. And some of them really don't like the idea of you being given the power to choose. After all, you might not choose them...

Lawfulness Of Processing

When another person or organisation (the data controller) wants to process your personal data, they need to have a lawful reason to do so. Without a lawful reason, they are breaking the law.

Processing should be lawful to the extent that at least one of the following applies:

a) The data subject has given consent to the processing of his or her personal data for one or more specific purposes

b) Processing is necessary for the performance of a contract to which the data subject is party or an order to take steps at the request of the data subject prior to entering into a contract.

c) Processing is necessary for compliance with a legal obligation to which the controller is subject.

d) Processing is necessary in order to protect the vital interests of the data subject or of another natural person.

e) Processing is necessary for the performance of a task carried out in the public interest or in the exercise of official authority vested in the data controller.

f) Processing is necessary for the purposes of the legitimate interests pursued by the controller or by a third party except where such interests are overridden by the interests of fundamental rights and freedoms of the data subject which require protection of personal data in particular where the data subject is a child.

Lawful Reasons For Processing Special Category Data

a) You have given your explicit consent to the processing of the personal data for one or more specified purposes.

b) Processing is necessary for the purposes of carrying out the obligations and exercising the rights of the controller or the data subject in the field of employment and social security and social protection law providing for appropriate safeguards for the fundamental rights and the interests of the data subject.

c) Processing is necessary to protect the vital interests of the data subject or of another natural person where the data subject is physically or legally incapable of giving consent.

d) Processing is carried out in the course of its legitimate activities with appropriate safeguards by a foundation Association or any other not-for-profit body with a political philosophical religious or trade union aim and unconditioned that the processing relates solely to the members are to former members of the body or two persons who have regular contact with it in connection with its purposes and that the personal data are not disclosed outside that body without the consent of the data subjects.

e) Processing relates to Personal data which are manifestly made public by the data subject

f) Processing is necessary for the establishment exercise or Defence of legal claims or whenever courts are acting in their judicial capacity

g) Processing is necessary for reasons of substantial public interest on the basis of Union or member state law which shall be proportionate to the aim pursued respect the essence of the right to data protection and provide for suitable and specific measures to safeguard the fundamental rights and the interests of the data subject

Allan Simpson

h) Processing is necessary for the purposes of preventive or occupational medicine for the assessment of the working capacity of the employee medical diagnosis the provision of health or social care or treatment of the management of health or social care systems and services on the basis of Union or member state law pursuant to contract with a health professional and subject to the conditions and safeguards referred to in paragraph 3

i) Processing is necessary for reasons of public interest in the area of public health such as protecting against serious cross-border threats to health or ensuring high standards of quality and safety of healthcare and of medicinal products or medical devices on the basis of Union or member state law which provides for suitable and specific measures to safeguard the rights and freedoms of the data subject in particular professional secrecy

j) Processing is necessary for archiving purposes in the public interest scientific or historical research purposes or statistical purposes in accordance with article 89 shall be proportionate to The Empress you'd respect the essence of the right to data protection and provide for suitable and specific measures to safeguard the fundamental rights and interests of the data subject

Your Rights As A Data Subject

To begin with, the GDPR gives you eight rights. Let's take a look at each of them now:

The Right To Be Informed

You have the right to be told about what is going to happen to your personal data: Which items of personal data are being collected; the purpose to which they will be put; how long it will be kept for; with whom it is going to be shared; the lawful reason for processing the personal data and how the personal data will be erased or destroyed at the end of the retention period.

Now, this right is often met by data controllers using a document known as a "Privacy Policy" or "Privacy Notice" which tells you about this. Some data controllers don't bother.

When they do bother, the privacy information is made available to you either in writing as a paper or online document, or orally over the telephone or face to face.

The right to be informed means they need to tell you what they're planning to do with your personal data. The GDPR even makes it clear how they should set about doing this.

Article 12 deals with **"Transparent information, communication and modalities for the exercise of the rights of the data subject."**

I'll paraphrase what it says:

"The controller shall take appropriate measures to provide and information referred to… …relating to processing to the data subject in a concise, transparent, intelligible and easily accessible form, using clear and plain language, in particular for any information addressed specifically to a child."

Which means you have got to be able to understand what they're telling you and clearly interpret what they're planning to do with your personal data. This is the only basis on which you can make a genuinely informed decision. I would argue that anything less is failing to inform you. Lawyers might disagree, but that's my opinion and I hold it for reasons which will become clear later.

What Does This Mean For You?

Well, you can tell a lot about a data controller by looking at their privacy policy or privacy notice. You can tell if they know what they are doing in terms of data privacy. You can tell if they are putting their own needs above yours as a prospective customer or employee. You can tell if their approach to processing your personal data is likely to be competent or simply half baked.

If they want you to become a customer, the privacy notice needs to inform you to such an extent that you want to trust them. If it doesn't, the decision about whether to go any further in the process is yours. It is your choice. You can choose to look elsewhere or to carry on knowing what you know.

Just remember that with these new rights comes a new responsibility. In this case a responsibility to make your own decisions about what you are willing to risk and what you are not. Probably with a view to reducing the risks.

If a data controller is deliberately obtuse and does not make it clear to you how your personal data will be shared - with other processors for example - and you still go ahead with a transaction which later brings harm to you, you had the opportunity to disengage at the outset. The alarm bells were there when clarity and transparency were not.

Having said that, you can still complain or take action in such circumstances because the data controller failed to uphold your rights on several levels. But why risk the aggravation?

Transparency means making it clear exactly where your personal data is going, who will be handling it and why. You might have had a bad experience with a particular data processor and you have no wish to repeat it. Transparency means you are informed and can make the decision to go ahead or not.

The data controller isn't obliged to tell you exactly who your personal data is shared with when they use a data processor. They can identify either the recipients directly by name (processor or 3rd party) or "categories of recipients". However good practice suggests transparency means naming them. If they don't name them you should be wondering why.

This right to be informed also means you have the right to ask a data controller if they are holding any personal data about you. The data controller is obliged to respond to you with a yes or no answer. Which leads us on to the next right.

The Right Of Access

You have the right to see what personal data a data controller is holding about you. The mechanism for this is known as a "Subject Access Request" (SAR) or "Data Subject Access Request (DSAR), which are the same thing.

Somewhere on the privacy policy or privacy notice there should be a section about your rights and how to exercise them, which will be a form or a link to a form or a downloadable document to use to make your Data Subject Access Request.

When you make a data subject access request, the data controller is obliged to respond, *"without undue delay and in any event within one month of receipt of the request"*.

The data controller can extend this period by a further two months if they are dealing with a complex request or a large number of requests, but they must inform you they're doing so within that first month and they must supply you with their reasons for doing so.

If the data controller doesn't take action as a result of your request, they need to inform you, again within one month from the data of receipt of your DSAR and tell you why. They should also, in this same communication, remind you of the possibility of lodging a complaint with the regulator (the ICO in the UK) and of seeking what's known as "a judicial remedy" through the courts. We'll come back to this last point.

Charging A Fee?

Normally responses to DSARs should be provided free of charge. This is a change from the old Data Protection Act which allowed an administrative fee to be charged. There is provision to charge a reasonable administration fee if the requests are, "manifestly unfounded or excessive", but if you and I are ever going to invoke a DSAR, we would be responsible about it and such fees would be irrelevant.

There are some safeguards built into this right from the point of view of the data controller.
They need to satisfy themselves you are who you say you are. Or in the case of a representative acting on your behalf, that they are authorised to do so. This is good, it means they want to make sure they're dealing with the right person.

Data Controllers are also protected against vexatious or frivolous attempts to use DSARs. Further, if your personal data is intertwined with that belonging to another data subject, the data controller is obliged to protect them too. In which case you can expect some data provided to be redacted or in some cases not provided at all if it can't be separated out. In which case they have to explain to you the basis for their decision. You still have the right to lodge a complaint with the ICO if you are dissatisfied and the data controller should be making this clear to you.

If these excuses don't apply, the data controller is obliged to make a copy of your personal data available to you. They need to do this securely, so this might involve giving you secure access to a website page which can only be seen by you, or in an encrypted format which can only be unlocked with a key (password) available only to you.

For some, this may appear to be a bit of a faff. Remember I said with these rights come responsibilities? One of your responsibilities as a data subject is to let the process take its course until you see the outcome. Let the data controller prove to you they are worthy of your trust. The good ones will respond positively. The bad ones less so. If you're not happy with the outcome, other options are open to you.

It is normal for the DSAR process to be carried out in writing (online or offline) as the Data Controller needs to have an evidence trail to prove their own accountability. It would be unusual for the process to be carried out over the telephone, although this does happen in some cases and indeed may be necessary depending on the nature of the issue involved. However you should be wary about telephone calls. We'll discuss this later.

The Right To Rectification

Mistakes happen. When you're giving your personal data to someone over the phone, it is possible they misspell your name.

As a data subject, it is also possible you make mistakes when you're completing data entry forms. Smartphones are great but they are responsible for all sorts of spelling errors (at least their owners are...) because of the "small screen, fat finger" problem. Or simply the smartphone user not concentrating on what they are doing.

In reality, there can be all sorts of reasons for a mistake with personal data. Records containing errors can cause expensive mistakes and missed opportunities for all of us. So it is in everyone's interest that the record is accurate.

Where you have an existing relationship with an organisation it is often the case you can make the corrections yourself in some sort of online customer or membership portal. Which means you can correct errors and update details as needed.

In other cases there can be errors of fact made by system errors or problems transposing data or associating data from other systems with yours.

As a data subject you have the right to make a data controller correct their records. Not just ask for it to be done, you can make them do it them prove to you the correction has been made.

The process for doing so will be similar to the DSAR. Many online systems actually incorporate the capability within their DSAR process. So if a company is taking your privacy seriously, they will have an effective means for upholding this right.

The Right To Erasure

During the run-up to the introduction of GDPR this was the right the news media fell in love with. "The Right To Be Forgotten". It grabbed headlines.

However now the GDPR is with us, the cold light of day reveals this is not an absolute right. Data Controllers can refuse to comply with your request. For example they may have a legal requirement to keep processing your personal data.

If they are still conducting business with you, you can't expect them to erase the personal data necessary for the purpose.

If they refuse your request, they need to write to you explaining their reasons. You still have the right to complain to the regulator.

If the grounds for refusal don't apply - and if you have reasonable grounds to ask for erasure - then the process will again be similar to the DSAR. In fact it will probably be an extension of it. You will probably have seen a process which looks a bit like this:

1. **Do you hold personal data about me? (Right To Be Informed)**
2. **Give me a copy of the personal data you hold about me! (Right of Access)**
3. **Erase all the personal data you hold about me! (Right to Erasure)**

To help you enforce your request and make it clear to the data controller you know what you're talking about, you might like to think about this in the terms used by the data controller and ask the following questions:

1. **How many copies of the data are there?**
2. **Where are they?**
3. **How will they prove they have deleted your records from every copy?**
4. **How will they delete your records from backup copies?**

5. How will they identify and delete your records from archived paper storage?

6. How will they prove they have taken all reasonable steps to comply with your request?

This "reasonable" word is going to crop up from time to time. If there are lots of legacy records involved or it is going to be very expensive or difficult to erase them they may not be able to erase everything.

You should also remember that complete erasure is just that. The organisation may be unable to retain enough information to prevent them from processing your personal data again in the future. For example if you make an enquiry with them again in two years from now.

The Right To Restrict Processing

That last point under the Right to Erasure is an important one. This right, the right to restrict processing, may be more powerful in some circumstances and of more use to you. It means you can tell a data controller to stop processing.

As with some of the other rights, GDPR does allow the data controller to decline a request to restrict processing but there must be a reason for doing so. For example in order to comply with a contractual or legal requirement to process the personal data involved. In which case the data controller is obliged to tell you exactly what the reason for declining is.

The GDPR (in Article 18) specifies four circumstances where the right to restrict processing applies:

A. The accuracy of the personal data is contested by the data subject, for a period enabling the data controller to verify the accuracy of the personal data.

B. The processing is unlawful and the data subject opposes the erasure of the personal data and requests the restriction of their use instead;

C. The controller no longer needs the personal data for the purposes of the processing, but they are required by the data subject for the establishment, exercise or defence of legal claims;

D. The data subject has objected to processing under Article 21 (Right To Object and automated individual decision-making), pending the verification whether the legitimate grounds of the controller overrode those of the data subject.

You can see how the right to restrict processing can be useful to you. Especially if processing has been carried out illegally. If you invoke your right to restrict processing the data controller cannot carry out any further operations using the personal data apart from keep it where it is. They are not allowed to delete your personal data in these circumstances and so evidence of wrongdoing can be preserved pending investigation. Assuming the data controller actually complies of course. However any subsequent investigation by a regulator or a court of law is likely to take a very dim view of such behaviour.

The Right to Object

In the following pages you will read about "lawful reasons for processing". Every processing action needs to be allowed by one or more lawful reasons, sometimes known as the legal basis for processing. One of those lawful reasons is called "Legitimate Interest". This is sometimes treated by data controllers (wrongly) as a bit of a catch-all - a legal basis to use when none of the others is applicable. I'll discuss this in more depth shortly. I think it is enough for now for you to know that Legitimate Interest can be used as a legal basis for direct marketing which does not use electronic media or telephone calls. It offers an "opt out" marketing communication regimen which permits ongoing direct marketing using techniques such as direct mail.

You should always be given the right to object and opt-out.

Especially if you want to prevent the use of your personal data for marketing purposes. In this situation the data controller is obliged to cease processing immediately.

The Right to Data Portability

You have the right to ask for your personal data to be supplied to you in a portable format.

This is to prevent unscrupulous organisations from trying to hold you to ransom if you want to change suppliers. Your customer history - for example use of household energy in the case of a power utilities provider - can be packaged up and supplied to you in a machine readable format so it can be used by your new supplier. It may not be in a format you can easily read, but the new supplier can.

Common formats are .csv, .xml. There are others.

Rights In Relation To Automated Decision Making And Profiling

As a data subject, you have the right not to be subject to a decision based solely on automated processing, including profiling, which produces legal effects concerning you or similarly significant effects on you.

There are circumstances under which this right does not apply, but there is condition which requires data controllers to make alternatives available to you. Let me explain:

This right refers to automated decisions. An example of this might be an application for a credit card, where the personal data you supply is subject to automated assessment by a computer. Ordinarily it wouldn't go near a human being before the decision was made known to you.

This right does not apply if the decision:

- Is necessary for entering into, or performance of, a contract between the data subject and the data controller; or

- Is authorised by Union or Member State law to which the controller is subject and which also lays down suitable measures to safeguard the data subject's rights and freedoms and legitimate interests; or

- Is based on the data subject's explicit consent.

In these cases the data controller is obliged to,

"implement suitable measures to safeguard the data subject's rights and freedoms and legitimate interests; at least the right to obtain human intervention on the part of the controller, to express his or her point of view and to contest the decision."

Automated decision making and profiling is used more and more in the modern data economy. You might recognise it in the form of Artificial Intelligence or AI.

You might also recognise the experience of a "doom loop" which can happen with automated processing where something you're doing doesn't fit perfectly into the design of the automated process. The results can either be damaging to you personally - by denying you access to something other people in a similar situation can access - or by causing you frustration as the automated system reverts to a default decision without taking your circumstances into account.

In cases such as these, a human intervention can be offered. Although you should be aware it may still result in the same decision.

What The Regulations Mean For Organisations and Businesses

Their Responsibilities

A lot of the responsibilities for organisations and businesses aren't new. They existed in previous versions of data protection law. What has changed is the weight behind them.

Where previously organisations, especially small ones, could get away with ignoring certain aspects of the law regarding the protection and privacy of personal data, now the risks are much greater.

The high profile change you may have noticed in the news media involved those fines. If the regulator ever decides to use them to the fullest extent they are serious. So whilst the risk for an organisation of "getting caught" might still be considered low, the outcome of being found guilty of breaching the GDPR is potentially a business killer.

Having said that, I once sat in an audience addressed by the UK Information Commissioner herself and heard her say those fines would be deployed only in the event of serious and repeated wrong-doing. They attract attention, but for businesses and organisations going about their daily business in a responsible manner, they are almost irrelevant.

A prudent regulator may choose to impose fines, but they are just as likely to issue an order to "cease processing" to an organisation in the event of bad things happening. The idea being to stop the rot and focus the minds on fixing things. Indeed the ICO has made it clear they currently see their role as more about supporting organisations to do data protection and privacy properly.

They understand these regulations can only work if everyone plays their part and that consistent encouragement beats threats most of the time. For all other times, they still have those penalty fines in their back pocket.

The regulator however is there to enforce the law. It is not really there to compensate you if your privacy is compromised and you suffer harm or loss as a result.

Which is why the GDPR (Data Protection Act 2018 in the UK) contains Articles 79, 80 and 82. These represent the second aspect of the weight behind the new data protection regulations: The fact that you and I and millions like us can use the law to force organisations to uphold our rights.

In a regulation containing 99 Articles, these little gems are buried close to the end. Which is perhaps one reason why the media hasn't really mentioned them. Let's take a look at the Principles which organisations need to observe first, then in the next chapter I will introduce you to the other rights you have, which nobody really talks about.

Principles Relating To The Processing Of Personal Data

The easiest way to present this to you is to quote direct from the wording of the GDPR itself:
Personal data shall be:

a) **Processed lawfully, fairly and in a transparent manner** in relation to the data subject. *(lawfulness, fairness and transparency principle)*

b) **Collected for specified explicit and legitimate purposes** and not further processed in a manner that is incompatible with those purposes; further processing for archiving purposes in the public interest, scientific or historical research purposes or statistical purposes shall in accordance with article 89 not be considered to be incompatible with the initial purposes. *(purpose limitation principle)*

c) **Adequate, relevant and limited to what is necessary** in relation to the purposes for which they are processed. *(data minimisation principle)*

d) **Accurate and where necessary kept up to date.** Every reasonable step must be taken to ensure that personal data that are accurate having regard to the purposes for which they are processed re raised or rectified without delay. *(accuracy principle)*

e) **Kept in a form which permits identification of data subjects for no longer than is necessary** for the purposes for which the personal data are processed; personal data may be stored for longer periods in so far as the personal data will be processed solely for archiving purposes in the public interest scientific or historical research purposes or statistical purposes in accordance with article 89 subject to implementation of the appropriate technical and organisational measures required by this regulation in order to safeguard the rights and freedoms of the data subject. *(storage limitation principle)*

f) **Processed in a manner that ensures appropriate security of the personal data** including protection against unauthorised or unlawful processing and against accidental loss destruction or damage using appropriate technical and organisational measures. *(integrity and confidentiality principle)*

What This Means For You

Lawfulness, Fairness and Transparency Principle

The data controller needs to have a lawful reason for processing your personal data and they need to make it clear to you what items of personal data they plan to use and how it will be processed.

Purpose Limitation Principle

The use of your personal data must be for a specific purpose. The data controller cannot collect your personal data for one stated purpose then apply it to another without first asking for your permission to do so. There is an exception here for historical archiving and statistical analysis, although these would often require the personal data used to be anonymised so it can't be used to identify you.

Data Minimisation Principle

The data controller can only collect the data they need to achieve their purpose and no more. The data collected should be adequate for the purpose and relevant. In other words they need to collect enough of the right data to get the job done, but they can't collect other items of data "just in case". There needs to be precision about what is needed.

Accuracy Principle

The data processed needs to be accurate. Which means accuracy at the point of collection and throughout the processing. For many organisations this presents difficulties. There can be errors introduced at the point of collection or processing by staff members recording the data incorrectly or simply making typing errors. There are also problems with data supplied by people like you and I using our smartphones. Data submitted using an online form on a smartphone used by someone with fat fingers travelling on a train or having their attention diverted while doing so can be prone to the most amazing errors.

There needs to be a way these mistakes can be rectified so data is as accurate as possible. Again, from our point of view as responsible data subjects, it is up to us to take care when submitting our personal data. However the data controller assumes responsibility for accuracy as soon as they collect it.

Storage Limitation Principle

The personal data collected can only be stored for a specific length of time. The longer data is held for, the more risk it is exposed to. This is why I talk about your personal data being "borrowed" by a data controller. They must not hang on to it permanently.

Yet the storage limitation timescale is not defined by the GDPR. Instead, GDPR allows other laws to define storage periods for the personal data involved. Where other laws influence the purpose of processing, they can identify the retention period. For example, "six years plus one" for business accounting records. However be aware of some organisations using this example as the default for all their personal data storage. This is not appropriate for other processing purposes where perhaps a year, months or even a few weeks might be more suitable.

Integrity and Confidentiality Principle

The collection, processing and disposal of your personal data is subject to a duty of care on the part of the data controller. They must ensure that your personal data is protected, safe and secure from influences internal and external.

For example the data controller must ensure your personal data is only accessed as required in the processing by authorised members of staff. Or that your personal data is not accessed and shared by third parties. Or even that it is not rendered inaccessible as a result of equipment failure or accidental loss or damage.

The Use Of Data Processors

Most data controllers use specialist data processors to help them with their processing of your personal data.

Which means they have to share your personal data with these specialist processors.

From email systems to customer relationship management, website shopping carts to accounting systems, loyalty cards, document management and mail fulfilment. The use of data processors is widespread.

Wherever a data controller doesn't have specialist knowledge available internally, it gets outsourced to a data processor.

But here's the thing:

Just as the data controller acknowledges they are not the expert and contracts with a 3rd party who *is* an expert, the GDPR makes the data controller responsible for everything. Including the bits they might know nothing about.
There's a fundamental contradiction here which can cause confusion.

What You Need To Know About Data Processors

The relationship between the data controller and data processor needs to be governed by a contract between them. This contract specifies how the processing should be carried out (in ways which uphold your rights as a data subject).

The data controller can tell you about the existence of data processors in their privacy policy. They don't have to tell you them by name but it is good, transparent practice to do so. This means you know who is processing your personal data. The data controller can categorise their 3rd party "data partners" instead of naming them.

Data processors are defined as working in compliance with instructions supplied by the data controller. If a data processor carries out processing of personal data outwith those instructions, they instantly make themselves a data controller in their own right.

Data processors can be in other countries outside the EEA. Some national governments take a very different view towards the privacy of personal data than those taken by EU governments. If your personal data is being transferred outside the EEA for processing, this should be made clear to you in the Privacy Policy. Together with measures taken to protect your personal data and uphold your rights, which may include what are known as "adequacy" decisions applied to certain countries (the USA and Switzerland being examples). You may not wish your personal data to be processed in certain countries.

Which means you have the right to object to such processing. However this may mean a vendor is unable to fulfil a contract with you.

Chapter 3

Realising The Value Of Your Personal Data

Personal Data. Did you know they've started to call it, "black gold"?

There is now enough value locked in to your personal data to attract the attention of those who want that value for themselves.

Some of these people and organisations are ethical about this - they want you as a customer, or perhaps your skills as an employee.

Others are not. They want your cash, they want to use your personal data to get cash, they want to isolate you, to embarrass you, or to use you to attack your workplace where they can find more data and other people to exploit

Both parties want what you've got, they just have different reasons for doing so.

Your problem is that they can often look very similar and you need to be able to identify imposters or take steps to protect yourself from them.

A New Gold Rush

So it seems the world is facing another gold rush. This time to exploit the value around personal data. History tells us every time there is a rush to exploit a resource there are far more losers than winners.

Of course the term "black gold" isn't new either. It used to reference the oil and petroleum so crucial to our economy since the late 19th century through to the present day. Our use of it since has produced by-products and outcomes we will be tackling for the next 100 years. From air pollution to unrecyclable plastic waste and microfibers. We are suffering from both intended and unintended consequences as a result.

If we are to benefit from the opportunities offered by the modern data economy, we need to learn from the past. I think we ignore history at our peril.

Instead of travelling hundreds or even thousands of miles over inhospitable terrain carrying the shovels and picks they'd use to blister their hands digging into the cold, hard ground, your modern-day prospector is different.

They can be dressed in a sharp suit sitting in a glass-walled office, or they might be sat in their underpants on the edge of their bunk in a bedsit. Either way, they're using a computer to prospect for your personal data.

It is not hard to see who the present-day winners are. Google, Facebook, Apple, Amazon - all examples of gargantuan organisations built on the back of personal data belonging to you and me. These businesses worked out how to capture and exploit personal data during an era when regulation and control were relatively weak. You can't blame them for that. However they now own the route to the customer. To get to you and I as consumers, businesses have to go through them. This is just one example of how a Klondike situation can concentrate power and resources in the hands of the few.

When this happens the power often goes to the heads of the board of directors, where, ethically speaking, it can be a lonely place.

Newsflash!

Some companies are up to no good with your personal data. And you probably gave them permission to do it. Whether you meant to or not.

However, at last governments all over the world are taking notice of what the EU has done and they are implementing their own "GDPR style" regulation. The general standard of behaviour to which businesses and organisations, large and small, will be held to account is that much higher. And is going to get higher still if you play your part.

An Egalitarian Gold Rush

This time the gold rush is different. Instead of the resource sitting inert in the ground, waiting to be dug up and claimed by a new owner, this time the resource is already owned by someone. You and I - and people just like us.

The EU recognised this. Their idea is to put the power and control firmly in the hands of people who really own the assets. The assets of the modern digital economy are the pieces of information gathered from us, about us and around us. In terms of the disposition of the resource, this is much more egalitarian than a gold mine or an oilfield. Nobody else can legally own your personal data assets. The best they can do is borrow them for a while. In exchange for which you are entitled to expect some value in return.

Our personal data can be accessed both by those we would share it with and those we would not. So while we need to share our data if we ourselves are to benefit from simple things such as home delivery, cheaper prices, faster services and connection to our loved ones far away, we need to take steps to secure it from those who would cause us harm. Or to make sure that when someone else borrows it, we can get it back. In this regard we need some help.

As private individuals, you and I expect - indeed I think we are entitled to expect - a high standard of protection. We have laws, regulation, policing and enforcement to keep our communities safe. We have military resources to keep our country safe. Now, if we are all to benefit from the potential of the data economy, we need capable regulation, enforced to ensure everyone involved in processing our personal data lives up to their responsibilities.

Data breaches are no respecters of the size of a business. The threat of harm does not discriminate between one individual and another. Rich or poor, adult or child. Every one of us, as individuals and as members of a wider society, can fall victim to the outcomes of deliberate or accidental action. Whether caused by your local supplier or a multinational. It makes no difference. Harm hurts. Damage leaves traces. There *are* consequences.

What threatens us most is ignorance. In some cases *wilful* ignorance of what can happen when things go wrong with your personal data. The intransigence which refuses to change for the better.

When I first wrote this section I thought I meant ignorance amongst those who run and work in the organisations and businesses who want to process our personal data. However I have come to realise ignorance on their part is never more dangerous or effective in causing harm than when it is combined with ignorance on our part. You and I, as individuals, our behaviour can multiply our risk of suffering harm.

Harm – What Is It?

I'm using the word "harm" a lot here. What do I mean by harm?

For the purposes of sharing your personal data, here are three types of harm which could afflict you when it goes wrong:

- **Tangible Harm**
  - o Bodily harm
  - o Loss of liberty or freedom of movement
  - o Damage to earning power
  - o Other significant damage to economic interests
- **Intangible Distress**
  - o Detriment arising from monitoring or exposure of identity, characteristics, activity, associations or opinions

- ○ Chilling effect on freedom of speech, association, etc.
- ○ Reputational harm
- ○ Personal, family, workplace or societal fear, embarrassment or anxiety
- ○ Unacceptable intrusion into private life
- ○ Discrimination or stigmatisation

- **Societal Harm**
  - ○ Damage to democratic institutions (eg, excessive state or police power)
  - ○ Loss of social trust (who knows what about whom?)

You can see the concept of harm covers many things. It can also flow through you to affect other people or even national institutions.

There is much more to this than meets the eye. What I'm saying to you is this: If you are not careful, you can bring it upon yourself and the people around you.

We Have A Duty To Each Other

I first became involved in data privacy and protection after someone very close to me suffered as a result of identity theft.

If you have never had to watch as someone close to you folded in on themselves under relentless, silent attack from an invisible and seemingly unassailable source, you might not understand just how dangerous inadequate data privacy and protection can be.

I can tell you about the effects of misuse of personal data from my own experience. It is vicious. Even in apparently simple forms, it is indiscriminate and pervasive. It can influence your life in ways you never thought possible. It isolates, it causes fear and desperation. It rips the heart from your defences and can tear at your very soul.

Some Uncomfortable Reading

Too much? Too dramatic? Do I make this sound too serious for you? While everyone else bangs on *ad nauseam* about those fines, I present you with the reality. It only takes one careless moment. So don't think about the consequences of bad data privacy and shoddy protection in terms of millions of banknotes fluttering around. That's not reality.

Instead, think of it in terms of an elderly relative, sitting alone, sobbing quietly to herself in a dark, cold, flat. Penniless because some idiot felt it wasn't worth making the effort with data privacy. She is now paying the cost of their negligence with every breath she takes.

Or a teenager locked in a toilet cubicle somewhere. Frightened and alone. Contemplating swallowing the contents of the bottle of pills she holds in her hand. Simply because some fool was able to hack into her smartphone and share her private thoughts online amongst the people she thought were her friends.

These are the outcomes of ignorance when it comes to personal data. Ignorance makes people vulnerable. And it is the vulnerable who really pay the price.

High Level Ignorance

I am particularly disappointed when I read the carefully prepared press statements issued by the chief executives of large companies in response to their latest breach of personal data.

Carefully chosen phrases such as,

"It was only names, addresses and emails which were stolen" or,

"We can find no evidence that payment card details have been abused"

...each belie the fact that these people clearly have no idea about the consequences of their corporate failings.

An address or an email address might be all a data thief was waiting for to complete the set of information they need to launch an attack on an individual.

Email addresses are nowadays used as a "unique identifier" for everything from your Paypal account to your online banking app. Criminals spend enormous amounts of time and money to identify active, in-use email addresses. They can then use them to cross reference with social media accounts and other resources. Or they could simply add them to a database for a "brute force" attack where they use the tremendous power of copy and paste combined with computer processing to try to get into your online accounts through the front door. Minimal sophistication is required and the rewards are attractive.

And as for, *"...we can find no evidence...".* In my experience this is another way of saying, *"...we didn't look hard enough...".*

In most of these high-profile breaches what has really happened is this:

The data processor has just told everyone who you are. They didn't mean to, but they opened the door to harm and asked it inside. As a result they lost control of your personal data.

Some level of contrition would usually be appropriate, but the legal implications of doing so ensure apologies are minimal.

So in the end, it's up to you to tackle ignorance with some effort of your own.

We Have A Duty To Ourselves

The regulators who created the GDPR all know one thing is true. This regulation only works if every data controller plays their part and every data subject is aware of their rights and understands their own responsibility.

The best way you can make sure they play their part well, upholding your rights over your personal data, is for you to hold data controllers accountable. For you to make your decisions based on whether or not you trust them. To hold their feet to the fire if necessary. No access to personal data without accountability.

If each one of us takes responsibility for our own personal data and makes use of the new rights given to us. If we choose to work only where transparency and trust exist. Then we start to create the conditions where it is much harder and less lucrative to be a data pirate or a data ignoramus.

The value within our own personal data should be exploited by you and I as private individuals first. We should only allow others to tap into our value after they have demonstrated they are worthy of our trust. Even then the value is based on an exchange - every time we allow our personal data to be used, we make sure we get something in return. Otherwise, why would you bother sharing it?

So you need to be wary of sharing your personal data in a situation where there is not a clear exchange, where transparency isn't part of the offer and trust either doesn't exist or is in short supply.

If you don't do this, you risk falling victim to every personal data pirate, thief and ignoramus out there. You will by your own inactions become their rightful prey.

You Are In Control - You Choose

The GDPR does one thing extremely well. It puts you in control. However the slight flaw it suffers from is this:

You need to know how it works if you are going to take control and exploit it yourself. Much of this book so far has had to include copy directly from the wording of the regulation itself. Whilst this regulation is more accessible than most, there are still things to be aware of.

Nevertheless, the information is available to you. You are in control. You can choose whether or not you want to exploit your new rights to make your personal data safer. To safely extract value from organisations with which you really want to transact.

You have options to choose to adjust your "acceptable risk" profile in order to take advantage of a discounted service or a special offer. You shouldn't have to, but you can if you want.

You can choose to enforce your rights and make organisations uphold them on your behalf.

You can make them prove to you that they are worthy of your trust *before* you grant access to your personal data.

As a customer, as an employee or as a stakeholder in some other way. If data controllers want you, they are going to have to play by the rules

Passive Or Active?

Having the ability to use the control you now have is different from actually making use of it. This is another feature of the choice you have - whether or not to actually use it.

There will be times when you will use your new rights and times you choose not to. However you will probably want to put your new, heightened awareness to work straight away and keep it switched on all the time.

In which case the awareness of your rights and of the responsibilities of data controllers forms your first line of defence when dealing with data controllers. The willingness to invoke those rights is a choice you can make on a case-by-case basis, depending on how you are treated.

After all, life would become tiresome very quickly if you had to launch a data subject access request every day. The simple response to an organisation which isn't doing things properly is to walk away and choose a supplier where it looks like your data privacy and protection is at the heart of what they do.

At the time of writing it is clear a great many businesses have taken the view you will not be aware of their responsibilities and so you won't activate your rights in order to hold them to account.

Those responsibilities are there to help protect your rights (the GDPR refers to this as "upholding the rights of the data subject").

Indeed I formed the following opinion early on:

Allan Simpson

The GDPR will struggle to challenge shoddy data processing if you and I as data subjects go about our daily business in a passive way, blissfully unaware of what's going on. GDPR gave us rights but we can only benefit if we actively make use of them.

In this event, the GDPR is like having a big gun but no ammunition. It looks scary to begin with but soon the data controllers realise all the regulator can do is flash their big gun around - nothing much else will happen. Although occasionally someone might trip over it and get caught.

This has probably been the case to date. The big gun has been shown off, mainly by the media, to everyone with the threat of eye-watering eight-figure fines. However without data subjects using the GDPR to hold harmful and careless processors to account, there is no ammunition. Not unless the regulator themselves trip over it.

Yet the interesting thing about this "big gun" is that it can shoot ammunition of different sizes as it becomes available. Action doesn't need to be taken by the regulator (the ICO). Instead action can be taken by you and I. Initially in the form of a Data Subject Access Request (DSAR) but also in the form of legal action in your local court of law. Action designed to force a data controller to uphold your rights, and action to penalise them when they fail. All of which can be followed up by the regulator as they see fit.

There is also ammunition in the form of each of us choosing to deny the use of our personal data to organisations failing to implement the principles correctly. As we each decline on a personal basis you might think of this as a fairly low-calibre shot. Yet if each of us makes an active decision to decline, what it lacks in, "weight of shot" is soon made up for by, "weight of numbers".

This power to choose and control, backed up with your rights as a data subject, is your new Superpower.

The Self-Educating Data Subject

Some of the Data Protection Officers (DPOs) I have spoken with report the behaviour of some data subjects as, "self educating" in terms of how they make use of their rights. The more forward thinking of those data protection officers are delighted by this. They do all they can to make sure their organisations play a positive part in helping data subjects with their self-educating efforts.

They take the view that a positive engagement with you and I as data subjects can only be a good thing. Regardless of the purpose of the interaction.

Which means if you and I are careful about sharing our personal data, we can use this to improve our own understanding of how to invoke our own rights. If we're able to do this with relatively benign data controllers who make use of transparency and whom we are learning to trust, it means when it comes to dealing with less capable ones, we know what we're doing.

You may need this knowledge very soon. Many organisations have adopted a more belligerent, "them and us", minimalist approach to the privacy of your personal data. They'll only do it when you make them do it.

Transparency and Trust

Trust is in short supply. The incentive for organisations to play by those rules is currently based on punishment and restriction instead of the benefits of sharing, openness and long-term relationships.

Which means their deployment of "transparency" hasn't been particularly good to date. Those who understand the advantages of transparency in generating trust are starting to reap the rewards but they're not standing out yet. Perhaps the rewards are so useful to them, they're keeping it to themselves?

You can choose which organisations you want to take the lead. You can choose to reward their transparency with your trust.

The Nature Of Trust

Trust is going to be an essential ingredient in the modern data economy. If trust doesn't exist, the sharing of personal data is diminished. Sharing won't go away however. People will still need to transact, to buy things, to access services. Where trust doesn't exist, the value of the transaction between both parties will be dramatically reduced.

As a buyer, people like you and I will behave differently. If we can't buy in a trusting environment where we might be prepared to pay a little extra for safer, better or more attentive service, instead we will only buy at rock bottom prices.

Without trust there will be no loyalty. We will only buy when we have to, from the cheapest suppliers. This will be our response to the risks posed in an untrustworthy environment. If we can't reduce other risks, we can at least reduce our financial risk. Which means we will move from one supplier to the next as prices race to the bottom. Supplier margins are squeezed, service standards fall and a slow, agonising, spiral of decline begins.

As players in the data economy, our satisfaction and choices are diminished.

What Makes Us Trust?

Trust comes from many sources. Here are just a few I want to introduce you to:

Authority

Doctors, lawyers, police officers, firemen – professionals ought to be trustworthy. Their training, experience and role in society means that when we seek their intervention in our lives, initial trust is almost automatic.

Affinity

A shared background, experience or philosophy – We like people who are like us. We trust ourselves. When we identify people who share these attributes with us our immediate tendency is to trust them.

Credibility

A factual basis on which to build trust – For example is a person is clearly authorised and certified to be able to provide a service, or if a product carried certain safety or quality approval marks.

Longevity

If a person or supplier has been in the community or in the business for a long time and is well known. The fact they are still around must mean they're doing something right? Trust can be attached in such a situation.

The Problem With Trust

When we trust someone - and I'm talking in the context of trust with our personal data here – we create the conditions where a valuable transaction can take place between us. In some cases, the trust is unspoken. It's just there, as is the case when you call the police or the fire brigade.

There is another source of trust: Experience.

Your grant of trust to another party lasts only for as long as your experience of the relationship is a positive one. If this ever becomes negative, or even just "neutral", the bond of trust can be broken, regardless of the original source.

Which means trust can never be taken for granted.

You, as a private individual, need to monitor the conditions under which you gave your trust.

Those to whom you award your trust need to treat this with respect. Their working relationship with you is held together by trust. A transaction might take place and repeated many times whilst trust exists. It could even become automatic. Yet when trust is broken, it might never be repeated again.

Whom Should You Trust?

You will be using local, national or even international suppliers for goods and services today. Most of whom you trust because your experience of them has been positive.

There might be some you're not too sure about.
Trusting them on the evidence of their performance to date is all well and good. However there is now another dimension to your ongoing relationship with them: The privacy and safety of your personal data. This can change the basis of trust.

Regardless of authority, affinity, credibility or longevity, your trust with personal data demands evidence which suggests you will be sharing it with someone who can be trusted to look after your interests. Not theirs.

Evidence that your personal data will, on balance, be safer. Evidence can give you confidence. Before parting with your personal data, you should be looking for evidence it will be treated with respect - and if anything goes wrong with your personal data, that *you* will also be treated with respect.

Large organisations are already discovering how precarious their positions as data controllers can be. Global airlines, hotel chains, online vendors, social media companies. They all contributed recently to data breaches involving hundreds of millions of customer records.

These are organisations which should know better and should have adequate resources in place to take steps to protect you when something goes wrong. The fact that frequently these steps have been faltering and hesitant is not a good sign for the rest of us. If a large organisation can't look after us properly, what chance have we got with smaller ones? Especially when you consider smaller businesses don't have access to the specialist resources needed to protect our personal data properly.

Many smaller businesses either haven't bothered at all or are using sticking plaster solutions for issues demanding much more attention. If they really want your business in the coming years, they are going to have to do better. Much better. The personal data belonging to you and I, that's what's at risk. So if you want them to look after you, now might be the time to raise your standards when sharing your personal data and make them make the effort.

Your current suppliers can be totally friendly and efficient. On the basis of their delivery to you there is probably no reason to fault them.

But are they really looking after you? Do they look after the privacy of your personal data in a way which encourages you to continue to work with them?

A Word Of Caution

It is important nobody gets carried away here. Some businesses do a lot less processing of your personal data than others. Most are very careful. In many cases the nature of the data processing itself is very simple. I am not suggesting for a moment that you change your allegiance from your current suppliers to new ones just because you're, "not sure".

If you like what they provide you with and you trust them, by all means carry on. Just be aware that your first line of defence is your decision whether or not to provide your personal data. There are simple things you can start to look out for. Clues as to whether or not a particular supplier knows what they're doing with your personal data.

They can be as friendly as you like, but if they are incontinent with your personal data, "friendliness" isn't going to help you much.

Take a look at their privacy policy. Does it tell you what you need to know? What do they want to do with your personal data? How long do they intend to keep it for? The longer your personal data is kept, the greater the risk.

Know yourself what you are and are not prepared to provide. What you *are* and *are not* prepared to put up with.

Your Right To Compensation

In the previous chapter I mentioned Articles 79, 80 and 82 of the GDPR and I described them as "nuggets".

They represent your rights to take your own legal action against a data controller or processor who has failed to uphold your rights. This is independent of any investigation carried out by the regulator and can be used, "instead of" or, "on top of" such an investigation.

If you're going to take such action, make sure you use a lawyer who knows about data privacy and protection. It is specialised stuff. You can be sure the organisation you take action against will be using a specialist to defend them.

Your Right To An Effective Judicial Remedy Against A Controller Or Processor

You have the right to a judicial remedy if you think your rights have been infringed as a result of the processing of your personal data in non-compliance with the GDPR (Article 79). Which means if a data controller or data processor isn't upholding your rights, for example they ignore your data subject access requests or continue to process your personal data despite you withdrawing consent and asking them to stop. You can ask a court to enforce your rights.

Representation Of Data Subjects

In Article 80, the GDPR allows you, as an individual, to join with other individuals to take a collective action against a data controller or processor. Very useful if you are to take action against a larger data controller or processor who has affected many data subjects.

Your Right To Compensation and Liability

This is Article 82 of the GDPR. It is worded in such a way as to encourage data controllers and processors to take you seriously:

"Any person who has suffered material or non-material damage as a result of an infringement of this regulation (the GDPR) *shall have the right to receive compensation from the controller or processor for the damage suffered."*

It is the expression, "non-material damage" which is important here.

Not only can you now take action against a data controller or processor who causes you actual harm, whatever form it might take, you can also claim for other damages. For example, hurt feelings or frustration.

At the time of writing, no such cases have been through the judicial system in the UK. Which means it remains to be seen how the courts will view an appropriate penalty for a given type of offence.

However it is possible these Articles of the GDPR could open opportunities for law firms to sell their services to you. After all, many of them are looking for a new source of income as the Payment Protection Insurance (PPI) scandal nears its conclusion. If the damages awarded are valuable enough you may very soon be able to use them to uphold your rights.

It is clear a great many data controllers and processors have not yet put their house in order with regard to the protection and privacy of your personal data. Leaving plenty of scope for resorting to the law and a "judicial remedy".

Allan Simpson

Chapter 4

How To Protect Yourself

Be Safe

Don't make yourself an easy target. Simple "brute force" attacks are the most common cause of personal data loss. Online, this is the equivalent of a thief trying your front door, if it is unlocked and falls open, they are in. Take some time to put some locks on your digital doors.

- 2 factor authentication – Many websites now offer this to help with security. It makes use of a text message to your mobile phone or the use of an authentication app on your smartphone. Both generate a unique code number for you to use when you access the website with your username and password, to give an additional layer with a second, unconnected form of authentication. Hence "2 factor". It is highly effective in preventing access from random "drive by" attacks.

- Longer passwords – The longer the password, the harder it will be to guess. In an ideal world, passwords should be cryptic. However in a practical world it's handy to be able to remember them, otherwise we lock ourselves out of the resources we need. If you must use names of places, people or things try to mix things up by inserting capital letters and symbols into the mix. Never use your child's name or date of birth. In this regard, be careful what you share on social media. You would be shocked at how many passwords are made up of information innocently published online.

- Password manager – One solution to the problem of cryptic passwords is to use a password manager. These remember passwords for your favourite websites so you don't have to. Although you really do need to remember the password for your password manager… An advantage of a password manager is it can be used to generate very long, almost unbreakable passwords without you needing to know what they are.

- Authentication app – As used for 2-factor authentication. Microsoft and Google have their own versions. There are others, such as "Authy". They generate a code which changes every minute or so, for you to use. If you use one of these on your smartphone, do make sure your smartphone is itself password protected. You may have a similar device attached to your online banking account.

Never share personal data with someone who calls you. Hang up and call the company back. Don't believe the telephone number they gave you on the phone. Instead go to your last bill or the company website and use the contact numbers you find there.

Don't leave your payment card receipts lying around. Yes I know the payment card number is usually partially hidden, but is it worth the risk?

Don't sign up for services using your Social Media login. Do you know what data it's collecting?

I'll tell you:
Years ago I set up an online contest for one of my clients. It was simple enough, entrants were presented with an online form and entered their name, email address and selected an answer to a question. The data we were collecting was only name, email address, their answer, the time of their entry and the IP address of their internet connection.

However the form we used had a feature allowing participants to place their entry using their Facebook ID to complete the form for them. The example form looked simple when we enabled it and it appeared to collect only what we needed: Name, email address, IP address and answer.

As private individuals we tend to be lazy. Especially online. Lots of people placed their entries using this optional Facebook method. It took minimal effort and appealed to the lazy gene.

Imagine our surprise when we downloaded the list of entrants. Instead of a spreadsheet showing us five columns of data, we could see some of the entries had many more columns of data. It was telling us all sorts of information about the entrants. For example:

Their location at the time of entry; the manufacturer and model of the device they used; the operating system in use on that device; their Facebook ID; all sorts of information we hadn't asked for in the entry form. Yet it was collected anyway and given to us. The Facebook user account provided lots of information associated with the person who entered the contest.

We were so concerned we decided to stop using it.

When these Social Media logins are presented to you, they look like a quick way to register or login. That they are. However they are also collecting new data about your personal preferences and behaviours. Did you know Facebook has something like 150 fields of data about each user? How do you think they go about populating all that?

They don't ask you about it when you sign up. Instead they collect it while you use their system.

Be Aware

The digital threat is constant. The real power of digital is the ability to copy and paste. Which means if someone develops a system designed to carry out a particular type of attack, it can be copied many times. Which makes it capable of mounting the attack in lots of places at the same time and/or repeatedly.

Which makes digital threats very powerful indeed. They can exploit small weaknesses and distribute compromised personal data to lots of places at speed.

The crossover world between digital and analogue. It might be easier to think of this as digital exploitation masquerading as things your more familiar with. Such as direct mail or telephone calls. Scammers can make use of the more traditional methods to try to catch you off guard. The combination of something you have seen online or on the news, with a direct communication such as a letter or a phone call lends a certain relevance or authority to a scam designed to access your personal data or your bank account.

If you are part of a group of people, perhaps hundreds of thousands of you, involved in a data breach, be very careful about how you respond to phone calls and letters.

The fact that you are actually involved in an ongoing data breach can make you desperate for updates or news. Scammers can take advantage of this human weakness by appealing to your need for information, help and assistance. So they'll give you a telephone number to call or a website to visit which looks like it belongs to the organisation involved in your data breach. They will send you an email designed to look like it's from an organisation, they might even send you a letter.

You use the information provided to call or you visit the website. It's not safe. They'll take you from there... Organised crime can afford to set up a call centre operation with the sole purpose being to separate you from your personal data.

In these cases ALWAYS verify contact telephone numbers and website addresses offered to you. Go and dig out old correspondence from the organisation involved and check the number on that. Resist the temptation to use the automatic dialling feature on your smartphone. Don't click links on emails. Instead, satisfy yourself you're making contact with the right people. It's part of your responsibility to yourself. Criminals will take advantage of your lazy gene if they can.

NEVER call someone back from the telephone number they used to call you. Some criminals use techniques which mean when you end one call then start another, they are still there. If possible use a different device. At least try to wait a while before making your call. They're relying on you panicking and reacting instantly instead of making a calm, considered response.

Be Informed

Take a moment to understand your rights. You are now a powerful individual. You have the power to grant access to those vendors you trust and you have the power to deny or withdraw the use of your personal data.

If people want to deal with you, they need to earn your trust. I'm arguing that trust can only exist in a place where you are informed about what is going on in a transparent way.

Three Ways To Inform Yourself

1. **Know Your Rights -** There is an increasing amount of
   good information available from sources such as the ICO
   regarding your rights and how to invoke them. It is well
   presented and easy to read. They publish this stuff for
   people like you and I. Make use of it.

2. **Keep an eye out for news items** about what is happening in terms of threats and potential harms to you and in general (organisations are now obliged to report breaches of personal data which could bring harm to you). More information is now available to us about the type of threats involved and how you might protect yourself. Being aware of them helps you to recognise and avoid them.

3. **Examine what other people and their organisations want to do with your personal data.** Set your own standards for what you expect to see and how you expect to be informed and stick to them. Potential vendors who don't conform to your standards don't get used. This might sound a bit excessive to you, however even the friendliest organisation can be a data privacy disaster waiting to happen. You just need to make sure there's less chance of it happening to you.

What To Look Out For

How Easy Is It To Find The Word "Privacy" On A Website?

What you find in a privacy policy or privacy notice on an organisations website can give you clues about what is really going on.

Almost every privacy policy you will ever find on an organisational website now contains the words,

"We take your data privacy very seriously."

Whether they actually do or not depends on what happens next. There is a tendency for some organisations to try to be cute or glib about their privacy policy. This is serious stuff. If they are not taking it as seriously as they should you will soon know, if you have prepared yourself and you know what to expect.

Of course, if they didn't bother to make it easy for you and you had to make some effort to find the privacy policy or notice. Eventually opening it to be faced with, *"...we take your data privacy very seriously"*, what would you think?

If your response was something like, *"Not seriously enough mate."* - and you're already heading for the exit, then this book is starting to have an effect.

Common problems with website Privacy Policies or Privacy Notices

There is a difference between a Privacy Policy and a Privacy Notice. Yet the terms appear to be used interchangeably. What I'm about to share with you is my own interpretation of the difference between the two. It works for me...

A **Privacy Policy** is, as far as I am concerned, a document intended to be used to guide the privacy practice and behaviour within an organisation. It is most likely to be intended as a "legally defensible" document. In other words, it is the version a business will rely upon if a data breach ever lands them in court.

A **Privacy Notice** is a document intended to explain to you what is about to happen to your personal data should you choose to share it with an organisation. It is clear, precise, relevant and easy to understand. This last factor can make them really difficult to write, however it is also what makes them work if it is written properly.

Good examples of this are around us all the time. If you live in the UK and you have ever used BBC radio, television or online services, you will see references to their "privacy notice". They never mention a privacy policy. Although the Privacy Policy document is clearly referenced in the Privacy Notice.

I am about to share some examples with you. Examples which suggest an organisation might not have invested in upholding your rights as a data subject to quite the extent you might hope for.

Privacy Policies - Early Warning Of Attitudes To Your Data Privacy

Privacy notices (or sometimes privacy notices) are there to inform you about why the data controller needs your personal data, what they're going to do with it and how they will uphold your rights (protect you).

There are different ways for a data controller to inform you and do it properly. Here are some examples of when it goes a bit wrong. You need to be aware of these, they are early warning signs of trouble later on.

There Isn't One

This happens more often than you might think. If the website wants you to share your personal data and there is no sign of a privacy policy or privacy notice. Leave.

The Lazy - Using a "fill in the blanks" Template

Template documents do have their uses. However using them to shortcut an organisations' responsibility for looking after your privacy shouldn't be one of them.

Some data controllers have attempted to minimise their effort by "topping and tailing" an existing document. Usually by cutting and pasting their business name and leaving generic clauses in place. Where this is done by a lazy person, you will be able to spot it. The font is different, the size of the text is different, the space at the end of the pasted text is missing.

The question this should raise in your mind is this,

"What else did they not pay enough attention to?"
The use of generic clauses is also a giveaway. They are often an indication the necessary groundwork needed to protect you has not been done.

The Impenetrable - Written in legal language.

Impenetrable privacy documents happen when the legal advisor got hold of a perfectly good privacy notice and felt the need to turn it into a "legally defensible" document. You can understand why they feel the need to do this.

The essential truth however is this: If *you* can't understand it, you are *not informed*. You cannot make an informed decision.

The wording of the GDPR in this regard demands, "clear and plain language".

The Denial - Just Plain Wrong

Occasionally you will find privacy policies which are Just Plain Wrong (JPW). The business owners or management are in denial about their responsibilities or have chosen to misinterpret the wording of GDPR in order to avoid making too much effort.

These are really easy to spot. For example, on a website containing a contact form, a newsletter signup for and an online ordering system, you might find a policy document which says,

"this website does not process any of your personal data"

When quite clearly it does. Yes, they exist. They're Just Plain Wrong.

Allan Simpson

Alternatively, you may find a website where the data controller claims,

"we only process data you have given us voluntarily"

- as though this somehow absolves them of any responsibility.

They do exist, these JPWs. My recommendation is to WoB. Walk on By.

Too Much Information

Sometimes, and it appears to me that some sort of fit of pique was involved - the data controller feels the need to present you with ALL of the information on the same page.

If the page is presented with suitable navigation and links to points of interest to you, this can work very well. Using a "Frequently Asked Questions" type of layout can work very well, with clickable headlines, an accordion or tabbed layout revealing further information. Otherwise it ends up being a wall of text. As the reader you won't make it past the first paragraph. The information is there but it fails to be accessible. You are not informed.

The Peek-a-Boo

Some websites make it really difficult for you to find a privacy policy or privacy notice. Even if it is technically, "on the home page" why make it hard to find?

You may find one buried deep in the footer of the website, often linked using really small text. I've often wondered what the point of this is? It is the equivalent of a small child trudging away from his parents muttering under his breath after being told to do his homework.

If the data controller is making the privacy of your personal data a small thing on the website. Is the privacy of your personal data a small thing everywhere else in their business?

The Old Fashioned

Every Privacy Policy or Privacy Notice for an organisation based in the UK should now refer to the Data Protection Act 2018. This is the name of the legal instrument involved.

If it still refers to the GDPR only, the document probably hasn't been updated since the 25th of May 2018. At least, not by someone who knows what they are doing.

If it only refers to the "Data Protection Act", you should carefully check which one?

I'm not joking. You'll find current policy documents which actually refer to the 1998 Act. Which means they could be 20 years out of date. However there are many similarities in the headings and wording between the two, so it can be easy to be fooled.

Something Borrowed

I know you will find this one hard to believe, but some organisations have simply copied the Privacy Policy from their nearest competitor or a business they admire and used that. Instead of doing any actual work to make sure they can still uphold your rights.

These can be really entertaining. If you are at a loose end you can have some light relief taking the data controller responsible to task (as long as you're a responsible data subject associated with the organisation of course! We don't condone frivolous or vexatious activity around here). Let me give you an example:

I found one such privacy policy on a hotel website. It actually contained a lot of good information, but I realised I had seen a lot of it before in exactly the same format. It was exactly the same, word for word, as the privacy policy for a competitor hotel a mile down the road. Only the name and the contact details had been changed.

The problem was, this privacy policy contained a lot of information about the special category data processing carried out for leisure club members. Which involved health questionnaires and recording essential medical information. The hotel down the road has a leisure club.

The hotel which had copied the privacy policy *doesn't* have a leisure club. So in stating they were going to collect all sorts of medical data, they run the risk of getting themselves in unnecessary trouble. Their privacy policy claimed they processed special category data, (and in terms of guest dietary requirements it probably does) but the hotel might not have the systems or records needed to support the collection of other items of medical data.

From your point of view, if they borrow the policies and means to process your personal data from someone else, should you be letting them borrow your personal data at all?

The Weasel

"Weasels" is an expression used by marketing copywriters. They don't like weasels. It means the modification of a word to alter the impact of its meaning by softening it.

So, *"We carry out careful checks"*, is modified as, *"We **may** carry out careful checks"*.

You see how a weasel works?

It is perceived by some as a clever way of wriggling out of responsibilities. In reality it is obviously evasive and smacks of insincerity.

The forerunner of the European Data Protection Board (it was called the "Article 29 Working Party") recognised such behaviour when it issued guidance about how privacy documents should be written and presented. It specifically noted that word "modifiers" such as this ***should not be used.***

A data controller either DOES or they DO NOT. Words such as "may", "might" or "sometimes" have no place in the information they're giving to you. These words introduce ambiguity. You cannot make an informed decision based on an ambiguous statement.

If you try, your decision to enter into a contract or grant consent is unreliable. What exactly are you signing up for?

Offline

When an organisation asks for your personal data, do they tell you what they want to use it for?

You should be looking out for spoken or written information. Both are quite reasonable. Either a member of staff who talks to you about what is about to happen or a card is given to you containing the information you need.

In public, are you mindful of situations where your personal data could be at risk? When you arrive at a hotel or a car rental check in desk, you are often required to share several items of your personal data. Is this done with privacy in mind?

Do you walk the streets with your smartphone in front of your face? The likelihood is that someone will simply grab it out of your hand. No hi-tech involved. Your problem starts with the fact your entire life is probably on that smartphone. It won't end there.

Do you use your smartphone on public transport in a position where other people can see your screen? Or even worse, be able to hear what you're saying? Remember smartphones now come equipped with recording devices.

Chapter Five

How To Make Your Personal Data Work For You

Your personal data works for you when you can let others borrow parts of it in exchange for getting what you want.

Controlled Sharing - How To Get What You Want

When another person or an organisation wants to make use of your personal data, make sure they are absolutely transparent with you about what is going to happen to it.

If they can't or won't tell you, why would you want to do business with them?

The one thing you can be sure of is that your personal data has a value. You own all the value. If a data controller wants to make use of your personal data, they need a lawful reason to do so.

We briefly looked at "lawful reasons for processing" in chapter 1.

In order for your personal data to be processed legally, the data controller needs to identify an appropriate lawful reason for processing. Sometimes it's called the legal basis for processing.

As a responsible data subject, you're looking out for the lawful reason for processing your data. The information should be contained in a privacy policy or privacy notice. Some privacy notices simply regurgitate the contents of GDPRs Article 6 at you, which specifies the list of lawful reasons for processing.
I suggest this isn't of much use to you. Instead you want to know the specific lawful reason applied to the specific purpose of

processing involved. Which is an essential component of transparency. Once you know what you're looking for, you'll know it when you see it.

In terms of your role in the modern data economy there are four lawful reasons I want to focus on. These are the lawful reasons you will encounter on a regular basis and you need to know where you stand when they are applied by the data controller.

Performance Of A Contract

If you are buying goods or services this lawful reason for processing will usually apply.

It also covers the process leading to entering into a contract. Which means if you make an enquiry about a product, this lawful reason applies to the processing of your enquiry up to and including the point at which a contract is formed or you cease your interest.

It is quite reasonable for an organisation to follow up with you until you make this decision.

When you decide to enter into a contract, all relevant communication and processing involved is covered by the "performance of a contract" lawful reason. So you might expect to receive service messages from the vendor. You might also reasonably expect to receive marketing messages promoting similar or associated offerings from the vendor.

What you wouldn't expect to receive from them is information about unrelated products or services. This would be outside the scope of the original stated purpose of processing your personal data. If they want to add this new purpose to your data, they would need to ask for your consent.

You can choose to grant consent, or not. It's up to you. It depends on what you want.

Consent and "Opt In"

The rules for consent were tightened with the introduction of the GDPR.

If data controllers want to send you marketing messages by electronic means or by telephone, they need your consent to use your email address or phone number.

There are other situations where consent is an appropriate lawful reason for the processing involved. It is up to the data controller to decide this, and for you to agree and provide the consent.

Consent is based on being informed. Transparency is critical in helping you make your decision. There are conditions about using consent:

- The data controller must be able to demonstrate you have consented to the processing of your personal data with a positive action. Which means they need to keep a record of what you gave consent for and how consent was given.

- The consent information must be clearly distinguishable from other matters and delivered in an intelligible and easily accessible form, using clear and plain language. (if it isn't this is considered an infringement of the regulation and your consent is not binding)

- You have the right to withdraw consent at any time, this should be made clear to you and it shall be as easy to withdraw consent as it was to give it. A lot of organisations still have trouble delivering on this. You can give consent simply by ticking a box. Withdrawing consent should be as simple as unticking the box. In many cases it isn't.

- Your consent should be freely given. In other words it is not subject to an obligation on your part or forced by an imbalance of power (for example in a contract of employment).

All of which can be condensed by saying your consent needs to be: Informed, for a specific purpose, the result of a positive action, freely given and can be withdrawn at any time.

For marketing purposes, consent is considered an "opt in" method for building marketing lists. From your point of view you only grant consent in order to receive information of interest to you, for as long as it is of interest to you. Then you can make it stop.

Giving consent can be a simple as ticking a box on a signup form.

For special category data processing, "explicit consent" is required. In practical terms this would mean an online form with a data field into which you type your name, next to a tick box indicating your consent.

Legitimate Interest and "Opt Out"

Not all marketing processing relies upon Consent as the lawful reason for processing. If we consider "Consent" is to be used for "opt in" marketing communications, Legitimate Interest can be considered "opt out". In other words a data controller can use the Legitimate Interest lawful reason to send you certain marketing communications.

Direct mail is one such example. A marketer can send you direct mail to your home address as often as they like, until you tell them to stop. In other words, you opt out.

Some data controllers and marketers view Legitimate Interest as a bit of a catch all, to be used when all other lawful reasons for processing aren't appropriate. Watch out for this, because applied properly it is anything but.

If Legitimate Interest is to be used as the lawful reason to process your personal data the controller must first complete a "Legitimate Interest Assessment" (LIA) and Balancing Test. The purpose of the assessment is to create a written record of the purpose of processing, the reasons for using Legitimate Interest as the lawful reason for processing and to balance the legitimate interests of the data controller against your rights as a data subject.

They have to uphold your rights, remember?

This LIA has to take place BEFORE they actually process your personal data. They can't claim it retrospectively. It should contain a description of the measures taken to uphold your rights as a data subject. This can be as simple as giving you a clear opportunity to "opt out" of receiving any further communication from them.

Which gives you the choice. It could be some vendors send you information you might find useful. Especially if they made some effort to get their targeting right and they send you information you're interested in. This way you get to decide: Keep receiving it or make it stop.

If you want to see if a data controller who is using direct mail really has your interests at heart, ask them for a copy of their LIA and Balancing Test.

Some controllers are so proud of their LIAs they actually publish them on their website! Others don't. The last time I asked for one I was told they couldn't send me a copy, "for data protection".

Yeah...

Compliance With A Legal Obligation

The GDPR allows other laws to interact with it and gives them scope to operate. An example of using "legal obligation" as a lawful reason for processing would be in employment law. Where an employer is obliged to process your personal data in order to comply with employment, tax or social security laws.
Even with a lawful reason the data controller is still required to observe all the Principles.

One final note here: **Bear in mind that people and organisations operating outside of the law don't bother with**

any of this. You can't get what you want from criminals. At least, not in exchange for your personal data.

An Older Regulation

Privacy and Electronic Communications Regulations (PECR)

PECR dates back to 2003 and is, as noted earlier in this book, due for an update in the form of the ePrivacy Regulations. At the time of writing it isn't clear how long it will take for ePrivacy to take effect, so for the moment PECR is all there is.

It works alongside GDPR in regulating how electronic marketing messages can be used. Phone, fax, email, text message, the use of cookies and providing electronic communications services.

It is PECR that requires marketers to screen their lists against the Telephone Preference Service (TPS) to reduce unwanted marketing calls.

PECR also requires marketers to have consent to use email addresses belonging to consumers. Although it is the GDPR which defines what this consent should look like.

PECR also provides for what is known as the "soft opt-in" for marketing emails sent to existing customers. It concludes it is reasonable for a customer to expect to receive marketing information regarding similar products and services to those they already use from a vendor. As long as the vendor/marketer is sending you information relevant to your existing relationship with them and gives you an option to opt-out, there is a provision for them to use your personal email address. The wheels of commerce do need to keep turning after all.

If you don't want to receive any more emails, you need to opt-out or ask them to stop. The GDPR steps in at this point with its' requirement for marketing emails to be stopped immediately on receipt of the request.

What To Do When It All Goes Wrong

It Will Go Wrong – Keep Your Cool When It Does

With the best will in the world, one day, something will go wrong.

Your personal data will be compromised, lost, stolen, destroyed, become inaccessible, used without your say-so, viewed by someone who shouldn't be looking at it. You may or may not be aware of it. It might be a small incident, it might be a serious one.

However this happens, it starts off as a "data incident". Something unexpected or unplanned happened to it. What matters to you is the level of risk of harm to which you are exposed.

If there is a risk of harm, the data controller involved is obliged to tell you so you can take steps to protect yourself. For instance by informing your bank so they can block fraudulent payment card transactions.

If there is a risk of harm, timing and speed are important. The faster the response to a breach, the better. You want to reduce the risk. The data controller is obliged to report a data breach which risks harm to individuals within 72 hours of being told about it or being made aware of it.

How To Report A Data Breach

I'm talking about reporting a personal data breach to the organisation involved.

As a responsible data subject I suggest your first duty is to do what you can to help contain the breach. Running off to gleefully tell the regulator or tell a newspaper reporter isn't really the ethos I'm seeking here. I'm not saying don't tell the regulator. I'm simply suggesting it might not be the first thing a responsible person would do. Only the organisation involved is in a position to do something about the suspected data breach. The regulator isn't, it involves neither their data nor their systems. All they can do is contact the organisation involved and ask them if they are aware. Then they will advise as necessary.

From a "first aid" point of view, contact the place where you think the breach occurred. Although I accept there are organisations and situations where you might feel the appropriate course of action is to call the Regulator or a newspaper.

Personal data breaches are inevitable. You know this. Some of them will be identified by the organisations involved. Other incidents will only become apparent when they are spotted by outsiders. Whether they were caused by an accident or a deliberate act is unknown to us when we come across evidence of a suspected data breach. What matters is we take steps to report it.

Once you report a suspected data breach to a data controller, they have just 72 hours to decide if it is a "reportable" data breach and notify the regulator.

Some data controllers have a breach reporting system published on their website but as a member of the public you are not obliged to use it. Instead you can use whatever method you see fit. Given that a data breach might have serious implications, I suggest you choose something quick. Telephone the organisation or email them if they have an email address published for either a Data Protection Officer (DPO) or responsible person.

If The Breach Does Not Involve Your Own Personal Data

Give them as much information as you can about the nature of the suspected data breach. Where it is, when you found it, examples of the data you found. Anything to help the organisation identify if there is a genuine problem and what has gone wrong.

If they know what they're doing they should respond to you promptly asking for as much information as you can supply.

If they don't respond promptly, then you should be reporting the breach to the regulator.

If the suspected data breach doesn't involve your own personal data you might hear no more about it. Although it would be nice to think you would receive some sort of communication thanking you for your efforts.

If The Breach Involves Your Own Personal Data

If the suspected breach does involve your own personal data what happens next depends on the nature of the data breach and whether there is a risk of harm to you.

Many data incidents are quickly resolved with no risk to the data subjects. Where action needs to be taken to help you take steps to protect yourself, the organisation may contact you directly or, if there are many data subjects affected, take to news media or social media in order to get the message out quickly.

Sixty-one Ways To Look After Number 1

1. **Assume your security has already been compromised**. This is what proper security professionals do. Whatever you did up until now, assume it's not safe and take action to secure things. Start now.

2. **Lock it:** Desk drawers; filing cabinets; laptops, tablets, PC's; mobile phones. If there is a lock – use it.

3. **Understand your online presence:** Thieves and hackers will target your money, your data, your workplace. Make sure you know where your personal data is shared and deployed. All the locations. The websites you use, bank accounts, social media accounts, systems you use. It's your personal data, it is up to you to know where it is shared.

4. **Safe Online Shopping.** Do you really need to store your payment card details in online shopping websites? Of

course it makes life easier. For a hacker. If it is stored, it is at risk.

5. **Be careful what you plug in or install** – only attach USB storage media if it is your own. Be careful when installing browser apps or mobile apps. Pay particular attention to the permissions they ask for. Don't let anything become a search bar on your web browser.

6. **Not all friends are friendly.** Some social media friends are anything but friendly. The only reason they want to connect with you is to gain access to data they couldn't otherwise see. It might not be a real person. There are apps using the Facebook and LinkedIn APIs to acquire data about you.

7. **Real world, usable password protection.** Use a password manager if at all possible. Use the paid for version where you can. Free versions of all software are free for a reason.

8. **Antivirus software.** Install it. Use it. Use the paid version.

9. **2 factor authentication** - security layers make it progressively harder for the casual villain and dedicated hacker alike. 2 factor authentication represents one such layer. Enable it where available and use it.

10. **Check your balances and transactions.** Keep an eye on bank account transactions regularly. If you don't check you won't detect a problem.

11. **If it is important to you, protect it:**

    a. Email

    b. Online banking

    c. Paypal

    d. Amazon, Ebay

    e. Wherever your card details are stored - do you really need to store them there? Yes this is the second time I've asked you. It is that important.

    f. Wherever your sensitive info is stored: On your home computer, laptop, local storage drive, Dropbox account, OneDrive, GSuite. If you can get in easily, so can a hacker. If all they need to do is compromise one device to gain access to everything, you need to make some changes.

12. **Know About Authentication** - how to prove it's really you. There are three methods of authentication:

    a. **Something you have.** This can be a simple as a key. The key to your home for example, or to a filing cabinet. Bring this up to date and you have

RFID proximity keys, such as those used for access systems and even motor cars. Email address, the identity card for your work. A credit card in your possession and the account numbers written on it.

b. **Something you know.** Your password, PIN number.

c. **Something you are.** Biometric data, fingerprints, retina scan, face shape. Also date of birth, full name. Things about you which can't be changed. At least not easily.

13. **Biometric data** - fingerprints, face recognition, retina scans. This is classified as "special category" data. Yet it is used by some for fairly rudimentary purposes such as logging in to your smartphone or your laptop computer. What steps have been taken to prevent this data from being shared in an unauthorised manner? Unlike a password, which you can change if it is compromised, you can't change your fingers.

14. **Keep it clean** - a periodic spring clean of software, apps and websites used. If you're not using it, get rid of it.

15. **Never use someone else's computer** to log in to your secured websites. I'm sure your friends are lovely and

trustworthy, but their system might have keyloggers installed unknown to them.

16. **KNOW where your personal data is deployed:** As with point no.2 noted above, but once you have your list, review the following points.

    a. Know what each online account is for.

    b. Set strong passwords on them.

    c. Delete old unused accounts.

17. **Small "p" paranoia – be a healthy sceptic**

    a. If it sounds too good to be true, then it's probably not true.

    b. If in doubt, leave it.

    c. Don't give out confidential data unless you are absolutely sure what it's needed for and what will happen to it.

18. **Linkedin Connection Requests** - It's nice to have lots of followers but are they genuine? Your LinkedIn profile contains a lot of information about you.

19. **Keep your software updated.** Operating systems, mobile phone apps, office software. They are all updated on a regular basis to keep them safe. These updates are often repairs to the software as a result of flaws revealed by

testing or actual attacks. Out of date software can put whole systems at risk. Look at what happened to the National Health Service as a result of a recent ransomware attack made easy for the attackers because of the use of old, unsupported technology.

20. **Use Big, Hairy Passwords.** We all know "password1234" just isn't good enough. Neither are children's names or dates of birth. If you have trouble remembering passwords try using a password manager. These are apps which create, update and manage passwords for you so you don't need to remember them all. They will produce long, gobbledegook passwords. Just the thing you need.

21. **Protect Against Ransomware** – Ransomware is a nasty form of attack which places malicious software on a device or system. Usually it denies the user access by encrypting the data or the whole storage drive itself. It then demands payment of a ransom to get your data unlocked. *Never* pay the ransom. To reduce the impact of a Ransomware attack, carry out the following:

   a. Frequent backups to multiple locations. This will allow you to remove everything from the infected device and start again from a "last known good state".

b. Don't keep a single copy of vital information only on your computer, keep a separate copy in an unconnected, safe location and protect it with a password. If you can, encrypt it.

c. Don't unzip .zip attachments from senders you don't know.

d. Don't click links in emails from unknown senders.

e. Keep your operating system up to date.

f. Use antivirus software.

22. **Everyone is vulnerable** - understand this.

23. **Don't fall for phishing.** Know what a phishing attempt looks like. Never respond instantly to an email. Look at it a second time. If in doubt, ask for guidance from your email service provider.

24. **HTTPS** - Only give your personal data to a website with the url starting "https://". NEVER share your data with one starting "http://"

25. **Free software isn't free** - unwanted pop-ups or applications are bundled with it. Browser toolbars – do

you know what else it's doing? Uninstall rubbish - you don't need this stuff.

26. **Be careful what you share online.** Do you give away potential passwords in your social media accounts? (child's name, pet name, birthday, place of birth...)

27. **Email security**

    a. Account recovery information – If you haven't set this up, do it today. Keep this up to date.

    b. Recent activity – Be aware of recent activity on your email account. If it all looks like you did it, all well and good.

    c. Account permissions – You and only you send email from your email account. If permission settings are available to you, use them to deny access to others.

    d. App passwords – Some systems, notably Outlook, use app passwords to allow your email service to be deployed securely in other services. This is quite normal. Make sure these passwords are never shared.

    e. 2 factor authentication settings. If it is available to you, use it.

28. **Tackle Spam**

    a. Be more choosy about where you submit your email address (or even use a free one for the purpose of lower-level communications, never use your primary email to join unimportant websites)

    b. Unsubscribe from newsletters you don't read.

    c. Never click on links in spam emails.

    d. Never download attachments in spam emails.

    e. Disable the automatic downloading of graphic images in your emails.

    f. On social media, adjust your settings to hide your email address.

29. Good Security Habits

    a. Use antivirus software on all your devices

    b. Disconnect your computer from the internet when you aren't using it.

    c. Never share your passwords.

    d. Avoid using public wifi services (in coffee shops for example)

30. Smartphone Common Sense

    a. Turn on screen lock and use it.

    b. Use encryption to protect the content on your phone.

    c.   Turn off wifi and bluetooth when not in use (saves your battery too).

    d.   When installing an app, make sure you check its permissions.

    e.   Back up your data regularly to a separate device.

31. **Online Adverts** - can be subject to malvertising attacks, when malware is added to a seemingly legitimate advert. Use an adblocker.

32. **Social check-ins** - Think about it - check in at the airport as you leave for a 2 week holiday? You're telling the network your house is unoccupied for a fortnight. Why do you want people to know your exact location? It's all very well having social kudos but is it worth it?

33. **Secure Browsing.** Consider using one of the new breed of secure web browsers.

34. **Stay away from naughty websites.** You know the type of website I mean. They're just full of interesting things to click on. They can take you to all sorts of sinister places which could install bad things on your computer without you ever knowing.

35. **Browser extensions.** Some of these are very useful. Others can be downright dangerous. Be aware of what

they are really doing. If you are not absolutely sure, don't install it.

36. **Scam Awareness** - free, get rich quick, share this to win! All designed to attract your attention or get you to drop your guard. Ignore them. There are even GDPR related scams.

37. **Don't use your computer with an admin rights user account** unless you need to. Create a lower level user account to be less vulnerable and keep your admin account for when you need to tinker with your machine or operating system.

38. **Multi layered security** - nothing is 100% secure. Layers of security make life more difficult for attackers.

39. **Security risk assessment checklist**

    a. Information - what type of data do you have on which devices?

    b. What online accounts do you have and how frequently do you use them?

    c. What would happen if you were denied access to them?

    d. How do you keep sensitive information safe?

    e. Do you share files or devices? Who else has access?

    f. Do you have backups?

40. **Don't delay** - secure today

41. **Be careful what you click on.** Read it first. Look out for spelling errors and URLs with odd characters in them.

42. **Be your own person** - don't copy what other people do. Their attitude to privacy risk is their own. You need to set your own standards.

43. **Free software just isn't worth the risk.** Paid services should work on your behalf. Free services work on behalf of the vendor.

44. **Never trust your friends or work colleagues** with your security information. Then you can respond truthfully to the question, "have you shared your password?". I have lost count of the number of business places where everyone uses a shared password.

45. **Does your smartphone autolock?** Is it enabled?

46. **Cyber-attacks are constant and everywhere** - how does your security compare with this? Is it always on across all your devices?

47. **Laptop webcam?** Tape it over.

48. **Mums & Dads** - no awkward photos of your children on social media. You don't know where these images will end

up. If you think I'm being a bit of a killjoy try explaining to your teenager why their pals have got access to images you shared of your child running round the garden naked as a toddler. Some people are just nasty.

49. **Keep your Web Browsers up to date.** Software updates and patches are issued regularly to help keep you safe.

50. **Use multiple email accounts**: Separate work and personal, use a low level account for general newsletters, secure accounts for more important things. Consider using an encrypted email account with shared encryption privacy keys for your sensitive information.

51. **Social networks are not safe places.**

52. **Don't use unsupported software.**

53. **Beware of fake antivirus.** This often pops up as part of a response to a browser search or in an online advert. It is an example of the "malvertising" noted above. No matter how plausible it looks DO NOT click on it.

54. **You start *all* the purchase processes.** Only ever install software as a result of a sales/purchase process YOU started.

55. **Use remote device locator for your smartphone.**

56. **Cyber criminals collect and collate information about you.** The more they know about you the more plausible their attempts to trick you will appear. They can use some of the data they collected about you to scare you into providing more.

57. **Google account security check up.** Do you have a Google account? Use their own security check up regularly.

58. **Stop saving your card details** to your web browser.

59. **Understand the INFOSEC Triad**: Confidentiality, Integrity, Availability. (INFOSEC means Information Security... the vendors you choose to share your personal data with should be observing this.)

  a. **Confidentiality** - information should not be made available or disclosed to unauthorised individuals, entities or processes. (in taking the time to assess the privacy information provided to you, this is your own personal authorisation process)

  b. **Integrity** - Information should not be modified in an unauthorised or undetected manner. Data should remain accurate and complete from sender to receiver.

c. **Availability** - Information should be readily available when needed. (not much point in having personal data if you can't deploy it or access it is there?)

60. **Don't reuse passwords.** Yes I know it's hard to keep remembering passwords and coming up with new ones. However it could be that you used an old password on a website which has since been compromised and added to a database of known username and password combinations. You must never use these old passwords again.

61. **Banking Apps - check it.** Sometimes you can be diverted away from safe websites or apps to dangerous ones:

a. Does the website use encryption? (it should)

b. Is the URL correct and not mis-spelled?

c. Are there any unusual extra fields in the login process? (eg, pop up boxes)

d. Fuzzy images, poor spelling or grammar? All tell-tales of fake websites and apps.

Security

You are up against everyone from rogue nations with their own massive datacentres to spotty children using a second-hand laptop in their bedroom. Some of these players can be highly motivated: If they want you, they'll get you. Some are just doing it for fun, getting a perverse kick out of upsetting people. The rest are just preying on the careless, witless and lazy.

As the owner of this book, you are obviously none of these things. So understand this. We are all vulnerable and we are all at risk. Yet we can reduce the risks dramatically by taking simple steps to look after ourselves. I've just given you sixty steps, some of which you can take right now.

How To Share Your Own Personal Data

Conclusion

How To Be A Responsible Data Subject

Your Choice, Your Decision

You and I are faced with a choice presented to us by the modern data economy.

This choice is *not* whether or not to take part. Governments and large organisations have arranged matters so it is very difficult *not* to take part. It is not impossible, but it is certainly time consuming and increasingly expensive, as older members of our society are discovering. Local bank and Post Office branches are closing. Access to these services is increasingly digital or not at all.

This is just one example of the way the modern data economy is moving. With the occasional, some might say "refreshing" analogue revolt.

There are still occasions where analogue adds value to an exchange of data. Although nowadays it is likely to be intertwined with digital.

Almost everything today is skewed towards the use of personal data in a digital format, at least in part.

Yet digital, as we have discussed in this book, is fraught with danger. The processing of personal data using intertwined digital and analogue systems means this danger can manifest itself in ways designed to trick the unwary.

Which brings us back to the true nature of the choice you need to make.

You can choose to take part in the data economy in a **responsible way** or to simply abdicate your responsibility and carry on as a passenger.

This is your decision.

It is harder to take responsibility for your personal data and your role in the modern data economy. Simply protecting *yourself* will demand more of you.

The reward will be in continuing to be able to take advantage of the innovations and opportunities offered by the modern data economy. Not the least of which is the benefit of being able to choose to work in an environment of trust and transparency. With you establishing and maintaining control over your personal data. Which means you get to use it again and again to your benefit.

This environment of trust and transparency comes as a result of you exercising your rights to control how your personal data is used and in holding data controllers and processors accountable for their actions. Over time, if we each choose to play our part, we can encourage perhaps even force, the changes in behaviour we need from these data partners.

Those who chose to meet us halfway with demonstrable accountability will benefit from our patronage. Those who don't, won't.

Choosing not to take responsibility for your personal data exposes you to the risk your personal data will be compromised and used against you.

In the short term, your life may well be cheaper and easier. However there are two big problems.

The first is that you increase the risks of both you *and those close to you* falling victim to the threat of harm as a result of misuse of your personal data.

The second is that you weaken the chain upon which we all rely as individual data subjects. We can do it without you but it will take longer. If we are to use our new rights to force lazy, inept and ignorant organisations to step up and play their part in the modern data economy, we need you.

How To Hold Data Controllers To Account

Know Your Rights

Your power as the owner of your personal data is given to you by your rights under GDPR. This power can be augmented by the regulator (ICO) and the courts. If things go wrong and you become a victim, these agencies can be put to work on your behalf.

Understand the Principles They Need To Observe

The Principles are important. They set the standard for how data controllers should behave. If you know what these Principles are, you can set your own standards accordingly and arm yourself with protective questions such as,

"Why do you need this piece of data?"

"Who will you be sharing this with?"
"How will you ensure it is kept safe?"
"How do you make sure it is only accessed by authorised personnel?"
"How will I know when you have finished using my personal data?"
"What do I get in return?"
"Who am I actually giving my personal data to?"

Insist On A High Standard Of Transparency

If there is no transparency about processing, what is the data controller trying to hide? There could be a perfectly innocent explanation, however the new Data Protection Act 2018 is quite specific about the information to be provided.

There is no good reason not to be transparent about processing.

Understand The Pressures Data Controllers Are Under

It is not just you and I who want to play in the modern data economy.
Organisations, businesses and other people do too. Most of them in a reasonable, benign and positive way.

For them to do so effectively, THEY need to demonstrate to the regulator and to you they are competent and can be trusted with your personal data. Again, this is all based on transparency.

What the Confederation of British Industry (CBI) recently described as, "the license to operate in the modern economy".

For any business to be sustainable in this modern data economy they need to conform. They need to work in such a way as to earn this license. It is granted by each of us as individuals, operating collectively.

Data controllers are in a position where they need to keep as many of us as happy as is possible for as long as possible. Which means creating and maintaining that "bubble of trust" and keeping us in it. One at a time.

They need to look after you. So reward them when they do. Withhold rewards when they don't. There's nothing wrong with you using "carrot and stick" to get what you want.

Reward Transparency With Trust

When you recognise transparency, understand it's there for a reason. The data controller wants to transact with you and they are doing it in a way which is a safe as they can reasonably make it. If they make the effort, the door is open for you to reward them with your trust.

Of course everything else has got to be right too – the product, the service, the price, the conditions, the terms of contract. But if you're faced with a situation where all these factors are the same and the only difference between competing organisations is trust, the safe thing to do is go with the one you trust the most.

If They Fail You, Invoke Your Rights

Some organisations take short cuts with transparency and trust because they think enough people won't bother or won't care and this will make their evasion worthwhile. These organisations will rely on individual sloth and ignorance if they are to continue to operate in the modern data economy. They put all of us at risk, but especially those who continue to transact with them.

With the constant threat of a data breach involving your personal data, it is likely you will experience a failure from one of your chosen vendors at some point.

How you respond to this is up to you. Most data incidents are fairly "low level". It may not be appropriate for you to throw your rattle out the pram with complaints to the regulator or threats of legal action. But it might be appropriate for you to ask the data controller to cease processing. Or for you to simply walk away.

High profile and harmful failings attract their own punishments. You can complain to the regulator, you can take legal action, you can join in a class action lawsuit now in the EU and the UK, as they do in the USA.

As individuals we only learn through making mistakes. Make sure any lessons learned by data controllers are not learned at the expense of compromising the privacy of your own personal data.

Have them learn at their own expense.

Hold them to account. Every time.

Your personal data is all about you.

The safety of your personal data depends on the choices you make.

Allan Simpson

Your decisions can never guarantee your safety. Yet good data privacy awareness can help you avoid the more obvious dangers and recover more quickly when it all goes wrong.

Hopefully, having reached this page, you are a little bit more aware of steps you can take to turn the modern data economy to your advantage.

Starting today.

About the Author

Allan Simpson works as a direct response marketer and data privacy practitioner. Nowadays there is plenty common ground between the two.

His companies operate data privacy support websites at On Data Privacy (OnDataPrivacy.com) and GDPR for Hotels (GDPRforHotels.uk). His marketing business is a member of the Direct Marketing Association (DMA).

He also works as the Data Protection Officer for a US based software company with operations across North America and Europe.

A member of the International Association of Privacy Professionals (IAPP), he is a Certified Information Privacy Professional (CIPP/E) and Certified Information Privacy Manager (CIPM). (*Allan would like to make it clear the opinions expressed in this book are his own and are not those of the IAPP.*)

He holds a BA Degree in hotel management and an MBA, the latter awarded by the Graduate School of Business at the University of Strathclyde in Glasgow.

After a career in hotel management, Allan has run his own businesses for nearly twenty years.

He is married with two grown up daughters and a grand-daughter.

He shares his personal data every day and worries about it every evening.

Mind you, he drives his poor wife mad.

Appendix – Examples Of Questionable Personal Data Processing

It is important you know where you stand with a data controller. Do they really know what they're doing with your personal data? If you do share your personal data with them, are they going to become a pain in the neck?

You want to protect your own precious resources of time and money. You want to save yourself from frustration and irritation. Above all, you want some reassurance they're putting your rights to privacy and your expectation of data protection above their own.

Sadly, this is frequently not the case. So I thought it might be useful for you to see what inadequate processing, which isn't meeting the requirements of GDPR and the Data Protection Act 2018, actually looks like. Or give you some examples of how you can exercise your own scepticism.

Marketing Signup Masquerading As A Contest

This is a common mistake.

An entry form for a contest or giveaway. In exchange for you supplying your personal data the organisation will send you a discount voucher you can redeem against a future purchase.

However you can't enter the contest or apply for the giveaway without agreeing for your personal data (in this case your name and email address) being added to a marketing list. If this was a consent box allowing the contest entry or the giveaway processing to happen, this would be fine. However the form wants to do something else:

If we leave the checkbox for, "I would like to be added to the … mailing list" unchecked as is the case here, the form cannot be sent, telling us, "this field is required".

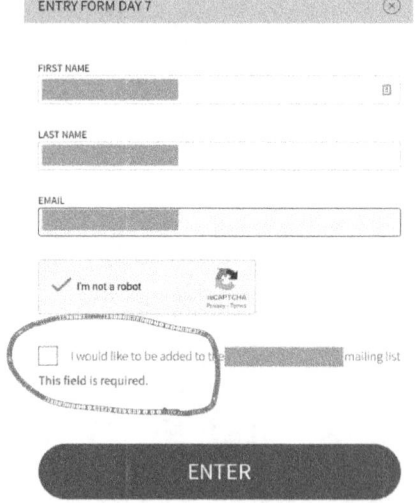

In order to be added to the mailing list with valid consent, your consent needs to be:

- Clearly distinguishable from other matters.

- Freely given.

- Indicated by a positive action.

There are in fact two processing activities going on here:

1. A Contest or Giveaway promotion, where you enter your personal data in order to receive the giveaway in return.

2. Processing intended to collect your email address for the purpose of future marketing messages.

It is quite reasonable for the contest or giveaway to ask for your personal data in order to be able to inform you if you have won, or to share the giveaway item with you. This appears to be the purpose of processing involved.

However the second purpose of processing – adding your personal data to a list for future marketing communication – is clearly attached to the first.

The intent behind the contest or giveaway is to capture your email address for marketing purposes. The apparent purpose of the form is only to allow you to enter a contest or receive a giveaway. In fact the two are combined.

In entering the contest you are being forced to agree to give consent for future marketing to be sent to your email address.

The request for marketing consent is not clearly distinguishable from the contest itself.
You cannot enter the contest without giving consent for future marketing, therefore your consent is not freely given. Which means the data controller does not have valid consent to send you future email marketing. It won't stop them. So the next mailing you get you can complain about.

Also, your right to withdraw consent is not made clear to you at the point of data collection.

This contest ran using a system operated by a 3rd party data processor. I am familiar with this particular system and I know they take great care to make their processing GDPR compliant. However in this case it appears their system has been badly configured by the user themselves.

A quick look at the website privacy policy for this particular business revealed clear gaps in their understanding of their GDPR responsibilities.

Allan Simpson

Telephone Calls Asking You To Confirm Your Personal Data

You need to be very wary of anyone telephoning you to discuss any of your personal data. You are not guaranteed to be speaking to a trusted source.

There was an insurance company which used to contact me by telephone.

They would identify the name of the company and ask for me by name. When I confirmed I answered to the name they provided, they then told me they would have to "take me through security and data protection".

Now, I understand their need to verify I was who I claimed to be. However the caller then proceeded to ask me questions such as my date of birth, mothers' maiden name and so on. All of which I felt disinclined to answer. After all, I had no way of verifying their true identity!

When I mentioned this to the caller and asked her how she planned to prove where she was calling from, she sounded a bit perplexed. This wasn't in her script.

Eventually she blurted out she couldn't give out any more information, "for data protection". Then she said they'd send me a letter instead and hung up.

It was likely to be a legitimate telephone call but the way the world works today, I would be reluctant to take part in a telephone conversation of this nature if it was started by someone else.

A sales conversation is fine by me if I can spare the time, but as soon as the caller asks for personal data it's time to end the call.

If there is a good reason for such a call, a reputable data controller will have a reliable system to verify your identity – and theirs.

Email Inviting You To Click On A Link

You receive an email out of the blue, apparently from a reliable source known to you, inviting you to click on a link to access your user account, perform a password reset or some other similar function.

Either don't click on the link or make sure you examine it carefully before you do click on it. It might try to take you to a website page controlled by a third party.

A password reset should be initiated by you and you alone.

If you need to log in to a website, just type in the primary website URL and follow the login prompts on the proper page.

Be very wary of anything giving you a link to follow in an email you weren't expecting.

Letter In The Post Regarding A Recent High Profile Data Breach

The news media delights in sharing the details of high profile data breaches with us.

In some cases, making use of the news and social media is the quickest way for an organisation to tell us we may be at risk of harm.

For example Marriott/Starwood, with their personal data breach potentially affecting 500,000,000 data subjects, would find it difficult to warn them all in a practical and plausible manner in any other way.

Which opens up the possibility of this method of attack beautifully.

You see, in a population of 500,000,000 there are bound to be a percentage of people who are at the same time quite worried about what to do, relatively inexperienced in the use of online technology and anxious for advice about what to do next.

Marriott followed the standard formula of offering an outsourced credit checking service to everyone on their database, with instructions to seek more advice on the website pages created for the purpose.

What the criminals could do is this:

If they have the compromised data, they could send a letter out to everyone affected, pretending to be Marriott.

Such is the effectiveness of modern computer technology I could knock one together within the next 30 minutes. I'm sure organised criminals can pass themselves off as any business in a plausible manner even faster than that.

Even if the criminals don't have access to the actual data, they could have a pretty good stab at finding out who stayed at a Starwood hotel sometime in the last four years. Using all those shared social media check-ins for example?

Then they send a letter out, apologising profusely for the breach and making it clear which website page to visit and which telephone number to call to take up their free credit/security check offer and set up an account.

The criminals have the resources to set up a call centre to process such calls and use them to gather yet more personal data, possibly including bank account details. Remember, people are panicking, they are trying to take steps to protect themselves. These criminals are appealing to the lazy gene by making it easy for frightened people to take those steps.

You can work the rest out for yourself I'm sure.

How to protect yourself from this type of attack? We have already discussed it in an earlier chapter:

Cross check the advice you're given in any letter, telephone call or email communication with details you have verified for yourself.

Dig out old invoices or statements; do your own internet searches (don't click on any adverts though, it could have been placed by anyone) and verify the contact details you need to make sure you're getting through to the right people.

Big data breaches lead direct to criminal activity designed to take advantage of them. Protecting yourself from this form attack is as simple as checking for the correct telephone number and not believing what's written in front of you.

www.ingramcontent.com/pod-product-compliance
Lightning Source LLC
Chambersburg PA
CBHW071432180526
45170CB00001B/309